"Rabbi Rudin has opened a fascinating window into the Catholic-Jewish rapprochement of the past five decades. Both Jewish and Christian readers will come away with a vivid appreciation of how individuals acting decisively at pivotal moments can steer the course of history. Informed by his own involvement in parts of the story, Rabbi Rudin dramatically underscores the transformative importance of the Second Vatican Council declaration *Nostra Aetate* and the American contribution to its realization, making his book required reading in preparation for that document's upcoming fiftieth anniversary."

— PHILIP A. CUNNINGHAM
St. Joseph's University

"Rabbi Rudin makes a fresh contribution to the study of Catholic-Jewish relations by recounting the fascinating story of three churchmen. He demonstrates the particularly American character of their lives and work, shaped by the immigrant experience and the country's heritage of religious pluralism. A story that bears hope, inspiration, and challenge for the future."

— CELIA DEUTSCH
Barnard College

Cushing, Spellman, O'Connor

THE SURPRISING STORY OF HOW
THREE AMERICAN CARDINALS TRANSFORMED
CATHOLIC-JEWISH RELATIONS

———⟳⟳⟳———

James Rudin

WILLIAM B. EERDMANS PUBLISHING COMPANY

GRAND RAPIDS, MICHIGAN / CAMBRIDGE, U.K.

Published 2012 by
Wm. B. Eerdmans Publishing Co.
2140 Oak Industrial Drive N.E., Grand Rapids, Michigan 49505 /
P.O. Box 163, Cambridge CB3 9PU U.K.

Printed in the United States of America

17 16 15 14 13 12   7 6 5 4 3 2 1

Library of Congress Cataloging-in-Publication Data

Rudin, A. James (Arnold James), 1934-
Cushing, Spellman, O'Connor: the surprising story of how three
American cardinals transformed Catholic-Jewish relations / James Rudin.
p.   cm.
ISBN 978-0-8028-6567-0 (pbk.: alk. paper)
1. Judaism — Relations — Catholic Church. 2. Catholic Church — Relations —
Judaism. 3. Cushing, Richard, 1895-1970. 4. Spellman, Francis, 1889-1967.
5. O'Connor, John J. (John Joseph), 1920-2000. 6. Judaism — United States —
History — 20th century. 7. Catholic Church — United States — History —
20th century. 8. Christianity and antisemitism — History. 9. United States —
Ethnic relations. 10. Vatican Council (2nd: 1962-1965)   I. Title.

BM535.R755   2012
261.2'60973 — dc23

2011038402

www.eerdmans.com

Contents

Acknowledgments

I could not have written this book without the guidance, support, cooperation, and inspiration of many people and institutions.

I am appreciative of the staffs of the Sanibel Island, Florida, Public Library and the New York Society Library in New York City. Both libraries provided superb writing areas and extraordinary research facilities.

I am especially indebted to Martin S. Kaplan, a brilliant attorney, an indefatigable champion of the environment, and a gifted leader in interreligious relations. It was Marty who inspired me to tell the story of the three Cardinals.

Another trio helped put this book together: my publisher Bill Eerdmans, Lutheran pastor and talented editor Dr. Norman Hjelm, and Richard Curtis, my literary agent. Linda Bieze, Jennifer Hoffman, and Andrew Hoogheem were excellent editors.

As always, Gerald and Deborah Strober, authors, publishers, and lifelong friends, provided encouragement and advice. Professor Thomas E. Bird of Queens College provided insights into the inner structure and workings of the Roman Catholic Church both in the United States and at the Vatican. Tom's remarkable knowledge and his sense of humor were invaluable.

Francis Lally, the Director of the Boston Archdiocese Archives,

and Charlotte Bonelli, who directs the American Jewish Committee Archives, were helpful in guiding me to the vast array of documents required to write this book. Professor Gerald Fogarty, a
church historian at the University of Virginia, supplied important
historical material and insights about the three Cardinals, especially Francis Spellman.

My many Jewish and Christian associates taught me more
than they will ever know, and I thank them all. The American Jewish Committee has long been my professional home, an honor I
never take for granted. Since 1991 the Religion News Service has
distributed my newspaper columns, and I thank the RNS staff and
management for that unique opportunity. It is my privilege to be a
founder of the Center for Catholic-Jewish Studies, cosponsored
by the AJC and Saint Leo University in Florida.

However, the views and opinions expressed in this book are
my own, and do not necessarily reflect those of the AJC, RNS, SLU,
or CCJS.

A quartet of amazing Jewish women has taught me humility
and provided enormous joy: our daughters, Rabbi Eve and
Jennifer, our granddaughter Emma Mollie, and my wife, Marcia,
who for more than forty years has been my loving companion and
constant writing muse. Because she is also an author, Marcia well
understands the effort and energy needed to turn a blank com-
puter screen into a book.

CHAPTER ONE

Surprise! Surprise!

———◈◈◈———

T his is the remarkable story of how and why an unlikely trio of American-born Roman Catholic cardinals — Richard James Cushing (1895-1970), Francis Joseph Spellman (1889-1967), and John Joseph O'Connor (1920-2000) — unexpectedly used the power of their high ecclesiastical positions and their personal charisma during the second half of the twentieth century to permanently transform Christian-Jewish relations and thereby change both Christianity and world history. That transformation remains the three cardinals' lasting historic legacy.

These events began with the efforts of Cushing, the archbishop of Boston, and Spellman, the archbishop of New York, during the Second Vatican Council in Rome, which took place between 1962 and 1965. They culminated a generation later with O'Connor, when he served as New York's archbishop. Even now, years after the deaths of the three cardinals, their extraordinary success continues to astonish many people, just as it did when they were alive.

Despite a shared commitment to build a new, constructive relationship between the Catholic Church and the Jewish people, the cardinals differed from one another in many ways, especially in their personalities and individual leadership styles. But, taken together, their achievements personify the Church's encounter with both modernity and with America's religious pluralism and demographic diversity.

Cushing was the gruff-voiced, earthy spiritual leader of the Boston Archdiocese from 1944 until his death twenty-six years later. Spellman served as New York's imperious, ambitious archbishop between 1939 and his death in 1967, and because of his global fame and religio-political power, which stretched from the White House to the Pentagon to the Vatican, he was often called "America's Pope." O'Connor, a career United States military chaplain, mistakenly believed the major part of his life's work had ended when, after retiring as a Navy admiral, he was appointed bishop of Scranton in 1983. But in fact O'Connor's most enduring accomplishments only began a few months later when Pope John Paul II named him archbishop of New York, a position he held for sixteen years, beginning in 1984 until brain cancer took his life at age 80.

Their achievements in Catholic-Jewish relations were particularly surprising given their backgrounds. Cushing and O'Connor were both children of Irish parents who had immigrated to the United States in the latter nineteenth century, and Spellman was a grandson of Irish immigrants. All were theological conservatives who grew up in a militant, triumphalistic church that over the course of nearly 2,000 years had developed a tortured and mainly negative history of relations with Jews and Judaism.

The cardinals were successful because they skillfully used a potent combination of personal audacity and a fervent dedication to ridding their church of the anti-Jewish bigotry that had poisoned millions of Catholics for centuries. In their efforts, Cushing, Spellman, and O'Connor were buttressed by an America whose longstanding ideals include religious liberty, interreligious amity, and freedom of conscience.

At two critical and defining moments in recent history, the three cardinals figuratively threw their red hats, visible symbols of their holy office and their individual prestige, into a series of major political and religious controversies that changed the Church's tangled, hostile relationship with Jews and Judaism. But it was not easy.

The dramatic and decisive interventions of Cushing and Spellman took place during the Second Vatican Council between 1962 and 1965, when over 2,300 Catholic bishops from all parts of the world came together to reform and renew the Church in response to the challenges of the modern world. The most controversial issue at the council focused on the Church's relationship with Jews and Judaism. Both Pope John XXIII (1881-1963) and his successor, Paul VI (1897-1978), strongly supported the passage of a groundbreaking declaration that addressed the issue. But despite papal efforts, by mid-1964 the effort was faltering as clerical foes of the proposed statement worked to block its adoption.

Enter Cushing and Spellman. Alarmed by the anti-Jewish attitudes and beliefs on display at the council, the two American cardinals made unexpectedly strong public and private interventions that guaranteed the council bishops would approve a positive statement. That declaration, called *Nostra Aetate*, Latin for "In Our Time," was ultimately adopted on October 28, 1965, by an overwhelming vote of 2,221 in favor and 88 against passage. Today, nearly a half century later, the Vatican Council's action grows in impact and importance.

In the 1980s and 1990s, a generation after Cushing and Spellman, and at a moment in history when the spiritual, psychic, and physical energy among many Catholics and Jews was on the wane after the initial early burst of excitement following the council reforms, it was John O'Connor who made real the interreligious promise of his two predecessors. He provided the world with the image and the reality of a prominent cardinal who placed positive relations with the Jewish people, Christian commemoration of the Holocaust, the fight against anti-Semitism, the freedom of Soviet Jewry, and support for Israel's security and survival among his highest priorities.

O'Connor stood on the shoulders of Cushing and Spellman and he became an international champion of improved Catholic-Jewish relations. O'Connor spoke often from the pulpit of New York City's famed St. Patrick's Cathedral about the radical evil of the Holocaust, the plight of Soviet Jewry, the Christian roots of anti-Semitism, and the need to stand with Israel. One of O'Connor's greatest successes came in late 1993 with the establishment of full and formal diplomatic relations between the Vatican and Israel, something he had advocated for many years.

But to appreciate the three cardinals' achievements, it is necessary to remember the way these two ancient faith communities — Catholics and Jews — had warily viewed one another for nearly twenty centuries, years filled with animosities and mutual suspicions. These American cardinals, each in his own way, had to confront and expose a long record of Christian hostility that included teaching, preaching, liturgy, hymnology, church architecture, and art directed against Jews and Judaism.

The three men publicly repudiated that dark underside of Christianity, the layers of bigotry and prejudice embedded within the Church that had for centuries been taken for granted by millions of people. Fairly common among these was the belief that Catholicism had fully replaced Judaism in the divine economy. Beyond this, there were aspects of religious anti-Semitism whose most obscene manifestation was the charge that Jews were a "Christ-killer" people, forever cursed by God as punishment for the "crime" of killing Jesus.

Challenging that negative tradition and seeking its elimination from the life of the Church required commitment and courage, attributes Cushing, Spellman, and O'Connor possessed in large supply. They needed those qualities and many others, including a generous dose of *chutzpah* — the Yiddish term for cheeky nerve or assertiveness — to achieve their difficult goals. Fortunately, the three cardinals enjoyed an ample amount of chutzpah as well.

4

CHAPTER TWO

The Way We Were:
Catholics and Jews in History

—◦◉◦—

T he fact that Richard Cushing, Francis Spellman, and John
O'Connor were able to transcend traditional anti-Jewish
teachings and move their Church and themselves into a new relationship with Jews and Judaism is a remarkable testimony to their
leadership abilities.

But as youngsters growing up within the burgeoning Roman
Catholic community in the United States, all three encountered a
basic Christian teaching that developed nearly two thousand
years ago during the early years of the Church: Christians had replaced Jews as the authentic "people of God." The ancient Hebrews and Israelites had once been a great spiritual people during
the period of the "Old Testament," the Christian term for the
books of the Hebrew Bible, but their divinely ordained task had
been fulfilled and completed with the coming of Jesus and Christianity. In order to better understand this narrative, and why it is a
false and dangerous one, this chapter looks at Catholic-Jewish relations over the course of history, starting with what we find in
the Bible and continuing into the modern era.

The Bible: From Abraham to Paul

Beginning with the patriarch Abraham as described in the book of Genesis (12:1) and continuing with Moses, the Hebrew prophets, and the 150 Psalms, the biblical people of Israel were the first to bring the concept and worship of the one God — what scholars of religion call monotheism — to the world. Central to the monotheism of the people of Israel were the Ten Commandments, a list of religious and moral laws meant to provide a framework for their worship of God and their treatment of one another. Pope Benedict XVI stressed the Ten Commandments as an important bridge between Christians and Jews in his address in the Great Synagogue in Rome in early 2010. He also said:

> [Today there are] increasingly close relations between Catholics and Jews. . . . [I]n the course of my Pontificate, [I] have wanted to demonstrate my closeness to and my affection for the people of the Covenant. . . . It is in pondering her own mystery that the Church, the People of God of the New Covenant, discovers her own profound bond with the Jews, who were chosen by the Lord before all others to receive his word. . . . The [Second Vatican] Council gave a strong impetus to our irrevocable commitment to pursue the path of dialogue, fraternity and friendship, a journey which has been deepened and developed . . . through important steps and significant gestures.

The Jews, as the people of Israel were known at the time of Jesus, provided the necessary religious environment, the required spiritual milieu, for his life and ministry, and later for the birth of a new religion, Christianity, whose roots go deep into Judaism. In his own teachings Jesus emphasized two other great commandments of the Torah (the first five books of the Hebrew Bible): "You shall love the Lord your God with all your heart, all your soul, and

6

all your might" (Deuteronomy 6:5); and "And you shall love your neighbor as yourself" (Leviticus 19:18).

Jesus was born, lived, and died as a Jew in first-century Israel (3 BCE-30 CE?), and his early followers were all Jews, including his mother and father, his apostles, his brother James, and the first fifteen bishops of the Christian Church. Jesus was executed in Jerusalem by the Roman Empire's occupation authorities, headed by Pontius Pilate, the governor of the region. For Christians, who revere him as savior and Son of God, Jesus was the Jewish people's single greatest gift to the human family. His life on earth was a divine reward for being faithful to the God of Israel — but once that gift was given two millennia ago, Judaism itself became a surplus religion.

With the rise of Christianity, Jews as a people — past, present, and future — were soon negatively portrayed as members of an oppressive, static community, burdened down by a heavy yoke of religious law, spiritually exhausted, and drained of religious vitality. It was widely believed among Christians that the Jews had performed their preordained mission of setting the stage for Jesus and his appearance in history. At the same time, Christianity presented itself as a universal religion that was free of Jewish "law." Instead, the new faith stressed the concepts of "love," "grace," and "compassion" in place of a supposedly repressive and discredited Judaism.

It was from the very outset an unfair comparison, a dangerous false dichotomy that produced horrific results in history. Instead of peaceful coexistence between two viable faith communities who both worshiped the God of Israel, the large majority of Christians operated on the belief that their new faith had fulfilled the role of Jews and Judaism, even going so far as to appropriate the cherished sacred name "Israel" for themselves. They were the "New Israel," successors to the "Old Israel"; for Christians, the Church had supplanted the Synagogue. However inaccurate, this disparaging view of Judaism resonated for nearly twenty centuries, providing powerful theological justification for negative teaching and preaching about Jews and their religion in churches throughout the world.

All Christians — Roman Catholic, Protestant, and Eastern Orthodox — revered the biblical Hebrews; they were extolled as exemplary pioneers of religious thought, and as the people through whom God had paved the way for Jesus. But in the nearly two thousand years following his crucifixion (a Roman form of capital punishment, as we will soon discuss) the overwhelming majority of Jews did not convert to the new faith of Christianity, instead remaining loyal to Judaism — which of course was the only religious tradition that Jesus knew.

Scholars believe Jesus was executed by the Romans in Jewish Jerusalem around the year 30. However, only a hundred years after Jesus' death, Christianity was already mostly Gentile, not Jewish, in its membership. The successful missionary work of Paul, known as the Apostle to the Gentiles, permanently shaped the demography of the new faith.

Paul was a Jew born in Tarsus (in what is now southern Turkey) around the year 5 CE, and during his early life he was known by his original Hebrew name, Saul. His father was a Roman citizen, a coveted and important status that permitted Saul to travel widely throughout the vast empire. As a self-proclaimed "Hebrew of the Hebrews," and a student of traditional Judaism, Saul was at first a fierce opponent of Jesus and his Jewish followers. But on a journey from Jerusalem to Damascus, Saul, who never met or experienced Jesus in human terms, encountered "Jesus, the Christ" (the Greek term for the messiah or anointed one, a redeemer figure long expected by the Jewish people) as a commanding voice from heaven.

His experience is described in the New Testament book of Acts: "Suddenly a light from heaven flashed around him. He fell to the ground" (9:3-4). Because the light was "brighter than the sun" (26:13), Saul was temporarily blinded (9:9), and a voice cried out to him: "Saul, Saul, why do you persecute me? . . . I am Jesus" (26:14-15).

Saul quickly abandoned his previous hostility to Jesus and for the rest of his life became the new faith's peripatetic leader, preaching the message that faith in Jesus, the Christ, was the way to gain eternal life and religious salvation. He was an ardent believer, and as a result of his conversion experience, he not only changed his name to the Latin Paul, but he also changed the nascent Church, moving it from a sect existing within Judaism into a new, independent, largely Gentile religious community.

Yet while Christianity began to move away from Judaism, the Jewish people continued to use the term *Notzrim* to refer to the members of the new faith — a term that continues to be used in Modern Hebrew today. This term means "Nazarenes" and is a reference to Jesus' hometown of Nazareth. *Notzrim* reflects the early Jewish perception of Christians as part of the people and religion of Israel, still members of the "House of Israel."

It was Paul who preached that faith in Jesus negated the religious requirements prescribed by the Torah, particularly ritual circumcision and the kosher dietary laws even though both were integral aspects of the Judaism that members of the Jerusalem-based Church — the original *Notzrim* — continued to follow. Paul's open rejection of much of Jewish religious tradition and observance made it easier for Gentiles, many of whom were unacquainted with or indifferent to Judaism, to become followers of Jesus. Yet it also made it easier to avoid the spiritual necessity of making the Torah the anchor and mainstay of their new faith commitment.

In his many travels to synagogues and churches in the Mediterranean Basin Paul stressed that belief in the divinity of Jesus as the promised Messiah superseded adherence to the demands of the Torah. But the Church nevertheless retained the books of the Hebrew Bible as sacred texts. They were the only scriptures Jesus knew, and his teachings were deeply informed by them. Yet in time new books — accounts of the life of Jesus and letters written by Paul and other early Christian leaders — came to be seen as having just as much if not more spiritual authority as the books of the Hebrew Bible. It is these works that Christians know as the New Testament.

Scholars believe that Paul was, like Jesus, also executed by the Roman Empire, possibly beheaded in Rome around the year 67 on the orders of the Emperor Nero. One theory is that the unstable Nero (who a year later committed suicide during a political coup) blamed Christians and their most visible leader, Paul, for the famous fire in Rome. If true, it was an early case of religious scapegoating — ironically, a tactic that Christians frequently used in later centuries against Jews and other perceived "enemies" of the Church.

In any case, that Jews remained loyal to their faith and traditions contradicted some major Christian beliefs and expectations. Throughout history Church leaders were disappointed that mass conversions did not take place, and, as a result, they often became impatient with Jews. All too often such Christian reactions created contempt and hostility directed against the kinspeople of Jesus. For many Christians throughout history, especially those engaged in missionary work, it seemed that the only acceptable Jew was a convert, one who was baptized and became a member of the Church.

It is not too much of a stretch to think of it as if a child first scorned, then hated, and finally attempted to destroy its parent. The initial attempt at destruction was by spiritual means through conversion, and if that tactic failed, then physical methods could be employed to assault and even kill recalcitrant Jews who remained loyal to Judaism, a religion most Christians believed was outmoded and spiritually inadequate.

There is a long record of Christian hostility and prejudice directed against Jews, who not surprisingly became victims of stereotypes and caricatures. For some Christians in history, the existence of Jews as a living faith community was an embarrassment, an unsettling refutation of Christianity's triumphant claims of supersession. The continuing existence of Judaism left Christians with a serious, even disturbing question: did the continued presence of Jews living alongside Christian communities in many regions of the world mean that the New Testament accounts, particularly those in the Gospels of Matthew, Mark, Luke, and John, were untrue?

"May it never be!" was the answer that came from Paul as he wrote chapters 9–11 of the New Testament book of Romans:

> I am telling the truth in Christ, I am not lying.... For I could wish that I myself were accursed, separated from Christ for the sake of my brethren, my kinsmen ... who are Israelites, to whom belongs the adoption as sons, and the glory and the covenants and the giving of the Law and the temple service and the promises, whose are the fathers, from whom is the Christ.... But it is not as though the word of God has failed. For they are not all Israel who are descended from Israel.... That is, it is not the children of the flesh who are children of God, but the children of the promise are regarded as descendants.... I say then, God has not rejected His people, has He? May it never be! For I too am an Israelite, a descendant of Abraham, of the tribe of Benjamin.... But if some of the branches were broken off, and you, being a wild olive, were grafted in among them and became partaker with them of the rich root of the olive tree ... do not be arrogant toward the branches; but if you are arrogant, remember that it is not you who supports the root, but the root supports you....
>
> ... and so all Israel will be saved....
>
> ... for the gifts and the calling of God are irrevocable.
>
> (Romans 9:1-8; 11:1, 17, 18, 26, 29)

However much he may have deemphasized the importance of faithfulness to the Torah, Paul clearly believed that the continued existence of Judaism was no threat to Christianity. But despite Paul's teachings, in the following centuries many Christian theologians called for greater conversion efforts to bring Jews into the Church; Christians simply had to try harder.

The Church Fathers

Many basic Christian beliefs and practices have been shaped by the teachings of the early Christian bishops and theologians known as the Church Fathers. Unfortunately, many of their writings exhibit a venomous attitude toward Jews, providing theological justification for anti-Semitic beliefs and attitudes. Much of the preaching, liturgy, and teaching of Christianity in its first few centuries stressed that Jews had forfeited their earlier vocation as a people of God, and that, as punishment for their venal complicity in the death of Jesus, they no longer retained the Eternal's blessing. Ultimate spiritual truth had been removed from them and permanently transferred to Christianity.

The writings of John Chrysostom (347-407), an early bishop of Antioch who later became a Christian saint, are among the bitterest descriptions ever written of Jews and Judaism. His words, including the charge that Jews are "Christ-killers," have often been used as a bludgeon to batter Jews. Chrysostom's *Eight Homilies against the Jews* includes this verbal torrent:

> [T]he Jewish people were driven by their drunkenness and plumpness to the ultimate evil; they kicked about, they failed to accept the yoke of Christ, nor did they pull the plow of his teaching. Another prophet hinted at this when he said: "Israel is as obstinate as a stubborn heifer." . . . Although such beasts are unfit for work, they are fit for killing. And this is what happened to the Jews: while they were making themselves unfit for work, they grew fit for slaughter. . . . Before they committed the crime of crimes, before they killed their Master, before the cross, before the slaying of Christ,

[Jewish sacrifices were] an abomination. . . . Nothing is more miserable than those people who never failed to attack their own salvation. When there was need to observe the Law, they trampled it under foot. . . . You [Jews] did slay Christ, you did lift violent hands against the Master, you did spill his precious blood. This is why you have no chance for atonement, excuse, or defense. . . . [T]he Jews are enduring their present troubles because of Christ.

Because of the widespread Christian belief that Judaism, after the coming of Jesus, lacked spiritual value, the Jewish post-biblical religious writings, especially the vast text of the Talmud that forms the basis for much of rabbinic Judaism, became objects of derision and defamation. Unlike the sacred Old Testament, which constitutes about 75 percent of the Christian scriptures, the Talmud merited little or no respect from Christian leaders. In June 1242, an astonishing twelve thousand precious, handwritten copies of the Talmud were publicly burned in Paris upon the direction of Pope Gregory IX; this was just the first of many burnings of Jewish writings that took place in other times and places.

Before the invention of movable type in the fifteenth century, which resulted in the widespread availability of books, the destruction of even a single handwritten Talmudic text was a horrific loss. The final redaction of the Babylonian Talmud, compiled by rabbinic scholars in what is now modern Iraq, took place in the fifth century. It is a huge work that in today's modern editions numbers nearly 6,000 folio pages, containing nearly 2.5 million words in 63 sections. Tragically, the recollections of those bonfires of hatred that consumed holy texts containing the name of God became inextricable parts of the collective Jewish memory bank.

Until the Second Vatican Council reforms were instituted in 1965, little if anything was taught in many Catholic churches, schools, universities, colleges, and seminaries about the vitality and richness of post-biblical rabbinic Judaism. Instead of a positive portrait of Christianity's "elder brother in faith," Catholic students of all ages and grade levels — including our Cushing, Spellman, and O'Connor — received negative or, at best, inaccurate and incomplete images and understandings of the Jewish people and their religion. Such instruction made an artificial and false distinction between biblical Israel (positive) and rabbinic Judaism (negative).

The charge of deicide, or "Christ-killing," was employed as a convenient religious justification to stigmatize, even persecute an entire people for all time, and not solely to demonize the Jews alive at the time of Jesus' death. Deicide, although never an official part of Church teaching, has had a gruesome, bloody effect upon its Jewish victims in many ages and many places. The sophisticated, carefully crafted theological delegitimization of Jews and their allegedly superfluous faith has been popularized and simplified as the belief that murderous Jews had been eternally cursed by God for killing Jesus. If proselytizing and forced baptism failed, deicide was readily available as a reason for punishing, even killing "stiff-necked, stubborn" Jews who would not abandon their faith and accept the new religion.

Pilate and Caiaphas: Reversed Roles?

A major source of the deicide charge emerged from the harsh New Testament portrayal of Joseph Caiaphas, the Jewish high priest of the Second Temple in Jerusalem during Jesus' lifetime. Caiaphas's image in the Gospels contrasts sharply with the more sympathetic portrait of Pontius Pilate, who was the Roman governor, or procurator, of occupied Israel from 26 to 36 CE. Caiaphas, appointed to his position by the Romans in the year 18, was always subservient to his imperial masters. However, in a momentous reversal of historical reality, he appears in the New Testament as badgering and bullying a bewildered, milquetoast-like Pilate, who is seemingly not the major power figure in Jerusalem. But, of course, he was.

In this distorted picture, Caiaphas and his priestly colleagues are the "bad guys" who seek the death of Jesus, and it is a weak Pilate who capitulates to the Temple-led bloodlust of the crowd and surrenders him to "the Jews" (a phrase used only sixteen times in Matthew, Mark, and Luke combined but an astonishing seventy-one times in John's Gospel). Pilate reluctantly orders the crucifixion of the charismatic preacher/teacher from Nazareth even as he literally and figuratively washes his hands of the entire matter.

Whatever theological or political ends this version of events may have served, it is clearly a case of turning history on its head, since the Jewish community, chafing for decades under the brutal Roman occupation, had no juridical authority or political power to execute anyone. It was only the ruthless governor, Pilate, who had that authority, and it is likely the Romans killed Jesus for the alleged crime of political sedition and not on the basis of any theological claims. Spiritual issues did not interest Pilate, who was contemptuous of both Jews and their religion. Like many other brutal rulers in history, what counted for him, above everything else, was maintaining personal power and preserving law and order in a restive province of the empire.

Historians generally agree that Pilate was the cruelest Roman procurator of ancient Israel, and because of his bloody record toward Jews — bloody even for Rome! — Vitellius, his superior, based in Syria, removed him from his post in the year 36, about six years after Jesus' crucifixion. Vitellius also stripped Caiaphas of his high religious office in the same year. Both men, forever linked together in the New Testament, began separate forced retirements: Pilate living out his life in seclusion and disgrace somewhere within the empire and Caiaphas, forced from his exalted position after eighteen years as the high priest of the Holy Temple, residing in the Jerusalem area until his death.

This raises an essential question: Was the portrait of the harsh Pilate deliberately softened by the writers of the New Testament in an effort to attract Gentiles, including Romans, to the new faith? And equally important, instead of Pilate, why was the obsequious and submissive high priest, along with all other Jews in history, made into the chief villains of the Christian passion story?

Not surprisingly, the Jewish understanding of this same story is radically different from the traditional Christian one. Jews have always affirmed their unique vocation of fulfilling the covenant their ancestors made with God at Mount Sinai following the Exodus from Egypt. Even many Jewish agnostics and atheists throughout history have believed Jews had a special role to play in history even if that role was not predicated upon a belief in the God of Israel.

From the Middle Ages to Modernity

Strengthened with that unshakable self-understanding, Jews have never viewed the development of the Catholic Church in particular, or of Christianity in general, as a form of divine punishment or as a judgment upon them or their faith. Indeed, several prominent Jewish thinkers, including the illustrious rabbi-philosopher-physician Moses Maimonides (1135-1204), accorded Christianity theological legitimacy; for him, it was a monotheistic religion whose followers remained bound to the God of Israel and a faith community with the potential to prepare the world for the Messiah's anticipated but long-delayed arrival.

Despite the statements of Maimonides and other prominent Jewish religious leaders about the positive role of Christianity in the world, Jews still had a difficult task relating to Christianity. They attempted to distinguish between the lofty moral and ethical teachings of the Church on the one hand, and the disdainful, often lethal behavior that Catholics and other Christians directed against theologically recalcitrant Jews on the other. Many Jews over the years have wondered which of the two is ultimately paramount in the Church, particularly in those historical moments when religious and/or political leaders carried out anti-Jewish actions or policies "in the name of Christ."

But overall, Jewish interest in Christianity has been peripheral; there are only a few references to the new religion within the enormous body of the Talmud. Faced with external hostility, Judaism turned inward; as a result, rabbis felt no need to encounter Christianity in any meaningful way. Besides, they were wary of any written discussion of the new faith, since religious and temporal authorities could interpret such texts as anti-Christian, a sure way to fan destructive flames of anti-Judaism among the faithful.

It is sometimes forgotten or overlooked that in the centuries before 1096, the start of the first Christian Crusade in Europe, there were many laws, ordinances, edicts, statutes, and decrees already in place restricting the lives of Jews and attacking Judaism itself. In 315, two years after making Christianity the state religion, the Byzantine Emperor Constantine decreed that Jews were forbidden to live in Jerusalem and forbade all attempts to convert Christians to Judaism. By 337 it was a capital offense in the empire for a Jewish man to marry a Christian woman. Among the many statements made by the Council of Nicaea, a meeting of Church leaders convened by Constantine in 325, is one that declared, "It is unbecoming beyond measure that on this holiest of festivals [Easter] we should follow the customs of the Jews. Henceforth let us have nothing in common with this odious people. . . . [O]ur worship follows a . . . more convenient course. . . . [W]e desire, dearest brethren, to separate ourselves from the detestable company of the Jews. . . . How, then, could we follow these Jews, who are almost certainly blinded?"

This same council formulated the Nicene Creed, which is still recited by many Christian churches to this day. Interestingly, one line of this creed acknowledges that "for our sake he [Jesus] was crucified under Pontius Pilate; he suffered, died, and was buried." But despite the recognition here of Pilate as the person who ordered Jesus to be crucified, and despite the prominence of the Nicene Creed throughout the ages, the charge that the Jews killed Jesus has never gone away.

Following Constantine's example, the Roman Empire adopted Christianity as the state religion in the fifth century, and in 415 CE Augustine, the Christian saint, wrote, "The true image of the Hebrew is Judas Iscariot, who sells the Lord for silver. The Jew can never understand the Scriptures and forever will bear the guilt for the death of Jesus." Three years later Jerome, another saint, offered up this description of a Jewish synagogue: "If you call it a brothel, a den of vice, the Devil's refuge, Satan's fortress, a place to deprave the soul, an abyss of every conceivable disaster or whatever you will, you are still saying less than it deserves."

The Crusades Begin

In 1095 Pope Urban II called for an armed crusade — from the Latin word for "cross" — that would free the Holy Land, especially Jerusalem, from the "infidel" Muslims. A year after the pope's appeal for action, the first European Christian soldiers and their ragtag followers began the long march from what are now Germany, France, and other nations to the land of the Bible, where they would fight to conquer the holy places sacred to their faith. But along the way, the crusaders perceived another target of opportunity long before they reached the Middle East and did battle with Islamic warriors: their neighbors, the "Christ killer" Jews.

One crusader wrote, "Great tracts of country stand between us and the enemies of God whom we wish to conquer. It is absurd to begin this enterprise when before our eyes are the Jews, more hostile to God than any other race." Most men who wore the cross made little distinction between Jew and Muslim. It is estimated that tens of thousands of Jews were murdered by the marauding crusaders as they marched across Europe. Atrocities took place in Cologne, Trier, Mainz, Regensburg, Prague, and other communities with large Jewish populations.

At the time of the Third Crusade in 1187, led by the famed English knight (and later king) Richard the Lionhearted, Jews in England were subject to physical violence. Perhaps the worst attack took place in March 1190 in the city of York. On the Sabbath before Passover, a group of Christian persecutors demanded a mass conversion. Many of the city's Jews fled to a fortified tower in the city for protection, but as the angry mob approached, most of the trapped Jews committed suicide rather than submit to forced baptism.

A century later in 1290, King Edward I expelled all Jews from England; they did not officially return until 1655, an exile that lasted 365 years. The number of Jews expelled from England in the thirteenth century was close to 16,000; many fled to the more welcoming land of Poland, which in time became a major center of Jewish life until the German invasion in 1939 at the start of World War II.

While there were ancient Jewish settlements in England and in what is now France, Italy, and Germany, the most famous and illustrious Jewish community was on the Iberian Peninsula, especially in Spain. It is incorrectly assumed that Jews first arrived in Spain at the same time as the Muslim invasion in 711; in fact, Jews had lived there even before the rise of Christianity.

Pain in Spain or a "Golden Age"?

Before 711, a series of Catholic-sponsored edicts subjected Spanish Jews to discrimination and persecution. However, conditions improved when Islamic forces gained control of the region. The

700-plus years of Muslim rule in certain provinces of Spain have been termed the "Golden Age" of Jewry, when followers of Islam and Judaism coexisted. It is certainly true that Jewish philosophy, literature, medicine, poetry, commerce, and biblical studies blossomed, but even during the so-called "Golden Age" there was Muslim-inspired anti-Jewish prejudice and bigotry. For instance, the family of Maimonides was forced to flee their native city of Cordova in 1148 because of Islamic persecution, escaping to Fez, Morocco, another Muslim-ruled area that was less hostile to Jews. Despite persecution, it is estimated that by 1300 there were 120 Jewish communities in Spain, with a combined population of 500,000.

Following their military defeat in 711, Catholics regrouped and slowly began the reconquest of Spain, one region or province at a time. By 1238, most of present-day Spain was under Christian rule, and the capture of the Granada area in the southern part of the Iberian Peninsula occurred under the leadership of the monarchs Ferdinand and Isabella, in the fateful year of 1492. It was the end of Muslim rule in Iberia. The Catholic *reconquista* brought disaster and expulsion for two faith communities: that year Jews were forced to leave the country, and Muslims were expelled later, between 1609 and 1614.

On March 31, 1492, the Spanish royal couple issued a lengthy "Edict of Expulsion" that called for the physical removal of all Jews from the country within four months. The document's crude and vindictive language reflects the traditional Catholic anti-Judaism that by the fifteenth century had infected many sectors of the Church. Beyond the traditional suspicions and prejudices, the edict is significant because it reveals a fear of Jewish *conversos,* the Spanish term for "New Christians," as opposed to "Old Christians" who were religiously "pure" with no Jewish family roots.

Baptized Jews were suspected of being insincere in their adopted Catholic faith, and the edict asserts that unconverted

Jews were "seducing" *conversos* and encouraging them to return to the despised Jewish religion. Indeed, that belief was one of the announced reasons for the expulsion of Jews from Spain.

Conversos often married one another, creating an additional source of "Old Christian" distrust. Sometimes, to prove their sincere Catholic convictions, *conversos* ate pork in public and exhibited intense enthusiasm in their Christian worship. But despite such efforts, New Christians remained under constant suspicion from Church leaders, some of whom were Jewish converts themselves.

Circumcision and keeping a kosher diet were cited as prima facie evidence of "Judaizing" by New Christians. Not surprisingly, they are the same visible Jewish practices that Paul had rejected 1,400 years earlier.

The edict of Ferdinand and Isabella threatened anyone who aided or hid any Jews who refused to leave Spain. As for the Spanish Jews themselves, they had only 122 days to prepare for their expulsion from a country where some families had resided for over a thousand years. They were permitted to "export their goods and estates" out of Spain — except for "gold or silver or coined money," in a familiar case of government expropriation.

The expulsions from Spain in 1492 and from Portugal five years later were human calamities that should not be underestimated or minimized today because of the even greater catastrophe of the Holocaust that took place nearly five centuries later. But the Holocaust and the earlier Iberian expulsions had one tragic thing in common: both the Catholic ruling authorities in Spain and the Nazis believed that blood, not belief, was the decisive factor in national identity, and Jewish "blood" was considered by both groups to be tainted, unclean, and a threat to their populations.

In 1449 a sinister term was introduced into Spain: *limpieza de sange,* or "purity/cleanliness of the blood." Fewer than 500 years later, leaders of Nazi Germany did not need to look far to validate their obscene views about the alleged inferior nature of Jews. Under the Nazis, blood trumped baptism, and Jewish converts to Christianity were still Jews and subject to the same persecutions that unconverted Jews suffered, including deportation and mass murder. The waters of the quickly dried baptism fount provided no safeguard or escape from the death camps' poison gas.

The Edict of Expulsion issued in 1492 included these grim words:

> There were some wicked Christians [*conversos* or New Christians] who Judaized and apostatized from our holy Catholic faith. . . . [W]e [the royal sovereigns Ferdinand and Isabella] ordered the separation of the said Jews in all the cities, towns, and villages of our kingdom. . . . [S]ince [they] have engaged in and continue to engage in social interaction and communication they have had means and ways to subvert and to steal faithful Christians from our holy Catholic faith. . . . [T]hese Christians hold meetings to teach their wicked belief . . . that according to their [Jewish] law that Christians and their children be circumcised . . . the fasts they must keep [Yom Kippur, the Day of Atonement] . . . having unleavened bread [Passover matzah] and meats ritually slaughtered [dietary kosher laws]. . . . [S]uch actions offend our holy faith. . . . [W]e banish the said Jews from our kingdoms . . . to depart and never return or come back . . . by the end of the month of July next of the present year. . . . [I]f they do not comply with this command and should be found in our said kingdoms . . . they incur the penalty of death. . . . [W]e forbid any person from receiving, protecting, or defending any Jew in public or in secret . . . under pain of losing all their possessions.

There were a large number of baptisms of Jews in Spain during the fourteenth and fifteenth centuries. Some Jewish conversions were sincere; others took place under duress and threat of death.

Conversion was perceived as a means of escaping the anti-Judaism that had enveloped Spain following the Christian military victories over the Muslims.

It is sometimes falsely assumed that the Spanish Inquisition that began in 1478 and lasted until 1834 and the Portuguese Inquisition between 1536 and 1821 were directed at unconverted Jews. It is true that the political and religious leadership in both countries expelled Jews, first in Spain in 1492 and then from Portugal in 1497. However, the actual targets of the dreaded Inquisition were *conversos* who were both psychologically and physically tortured in systematic and concerted efforts to make them admit they were still faithful to Judaism.

When *conversos* broke under such brutality, they were often forced to beg for penance in a city's major public square, a Catholic religious service called in Spanish an *auto-da-fe,* or "act of faith." In a bit of sophistry, once the public *auto-da-fe* was completed, the temporal authorities actually carried out the executions of the religiously "guilty." It was a clever way to separate the Church from the actual killings.

The expulsion in 1492 took place despite several vain attempts by prominent Spanish Jews to rescind or delay the stern edict. But Ferdinand and Isabella were intractable, and the queen was certain the expulsion reflected the "will of God." Some Jews fled to nearby Portugal, but in 1497 King Manuel I decreed that all Jews in his realm had to convert to Catholicism.

However, Jews from the Iberian Peninsula did find havens of refuge in some Muslim areas of North Africa, Protestant Holland, Catholic Naples and Rome, Eastern Orthodox Greece (especially in Thessaloniki), and Islamic Turkey. The assistance of the already established Jewish communities in those locations and the various rulers who welcomed the exiles is frequently an untold chapter of the Spanish Expulsion. Spain's self-inflicted loss of its Jews was "converted" into significant gains for other cities, countries, nations, and regions of the world.

Historical Anti-Judaism

We could name other examples of Christian anti-Judaism throughout history. There is the pernicious "blood libel" charge — the claim that Jews required the blood of a young Christian child for use in the baking of the matzah, the unleavened bread of Passover. According to the historian Walter Laqueur,

> there have been about 150 recorded cases of blood libel (not to mention thousands of rumors) that resulted in the arrest and killing of Jews throughout history, most of them in the Middle Ages. . . . In almost every case, Jews were murdered, sometimes by a mob, sometimes following torture and a trial.

Another ugly charge is "host desecration," in which Jews were accused of "wounding" the wafer used in the Eucharist service. The belief was that just as Jews wounded, pierced, and killed the body of Jesus during his lifetime, so they continued and replicated their ancient wickedness by somehow damaging the wafer Christians believe becomes (or, in some denominations, symbolizes) the body of Christ in the Mass.

There is also the infamous claim, made in 1348, during the worst of the bubonic plague epidemic in Europe, that Jews poisoned wells so Christians would be infected with the deadly disease when they drank the contaminated water. During that period Jews usually maintained a regulated system of personal hygiene for religious reasons; this routine included washing one's hands before eating, making regular visits to a *mikveh* or bathing pool, and the cleaning of cooking utensils. As a result, it appeared that Jews suffered less from the plague than their Christian neighbors.

When some German Catholic leaders asked the pope to support their scurrilous charges about the poisoned wells and host desecration, Clement VI's negative response included the Latin word *stupido*. The pontiff believed the accusations lacked any plausibility. Clement issued two papal edicts, or "bulls," in 1348 that accused Catholic tormentors of Jews of being "seduced by that liar, the Devil." The pope asked clergy to protect Jews from violent attacks, calling such persecutions "horrible" events. Other popes throughout history also denounced the blood libel charge, but despite their efforts to dispel such falsehoods, the pathology has nevertheless worked its way into the minds of many people.

Modern anti-Semites have echoed this charge many times in updated distorted forms; the latest example is the claim that Jewish doctors in the United States have deliberately infected African Americans with the deadly HIV-AIDS virus. Like deadly physical diseases of the body, obscene bigotry also mutates and appears in myriad forms and guises.

Even this brief survey of nearly 2,000 years of Catholic-Jewish relations indicates a complex history of both dark shadows and sunlight. It is easy and perhaps understandable to assume that anti-Jewish discrimination and prejudice have been historical constants. Yet the belief that all Catholic clergy, from local priests to popes, were uniformly hostile toward Jews and Judaism is wrong. As we saw with the example of Clement, there were instances when Church leaders acted with true "Christian charity" and compassion towards Jews.

But the overall record is a bleak one, and the pattern of *adversus Judaeos,* that is, religious anti-Judaism, within much of the Catholic Church did not significantly change until the Second Vatican Council. And even then it required three remarkable American cardinals to play major roles in the efforts to overcome the teachings of their own religious education and to break the pattern of Catholic contempt and hostility toward Jews and Judaism.

A Bitter Legacy

This was the bitter legacy Cushing, Spellman, and O'Connor inherited as young American Catholics. But as we shall see in later chapters, despite that tradition the three men moved their Church to a higher place and a new understanding and appreciation of the long-despised Jewish people and their supposedly empty religion.

Their accomplishments and the subsequent development of positive relations between Catholics and Jews since the conclusion of the Second Vatican Council is a great success story, a spiritual revolution of the twentieth century. There have been more positive encounters between Catholics and Jews since 1965 than there were in the first 1,900 years of Christianity. Cushing, Spellman, and O'Connor worked to replace a bad culture with a new positive one, and today's constructive Catholic-Jewish relationships, at once promising and fragile, are built upon the principles of mutual respect, knowledge, and understanding the three men championed.

The famous song from *The Fantasticks,* the long-running Off-Broadway show, asks, "Try to Remember." Christians and Jews need to remember not the way it was a thousand years ago, but the way it was only fifty years ago. Even in the United States, until recently most Christians and Jews lived in spiritual, emotional, psychological, and physical isolation from one another.

Before the bishops at the Second Vatican Council began their deliberations, there were skeptics in both communities who were convinced the painful status quo would continue indefinitely. They publicly scoffed at "naïve" Catholics and Jews who made efforts to change the old negative relationship, and they settled for a continuation of the hostile co-existence between Catholics and Jews, a cease-fire that was not a genuine peace. They believed Catholics and Jews were destined to remain religious adversaries.

But that deep skepticism was not shared in the 1960s by either

Cushing or Spellman. Nor did O'Connor accept the status quo in the 1980s and 1990s. Part of their optimism and success stemmed, of course, from the leadership of Popes John XXIII, Paul VI, and John Paul II, and from the support of other Catholic leaders. Yet their success was also made possible in part by the unique history of religion and state in America, which is the subject to which we now turn.

CHAPTER THREE

America, the Different

======*ᗧ∕ᗧ∕ᗧ*======

M any of the men and women who left Britain for its thirteen
North American colonies in the seventeenth and eighteenth centuries did so in pursuit of religious liberty and freedom
of conscience. The Anglican Church was founded in 1534 following
King Henry VIII's break with Rome, and after decades of struggle it
became the established Christian denomination in Britain. Part of
this process of solidifying its power included persecuting religious
dissidents, including Methodists, Quakers (originally a derisive
term for members of the Society of Friends), Baptists, and Congregationalists. Christians belonging to these and other minority
communities were intimidated and punished in secret tribunal
sessions without juries, public indictments, appeals, or witnesses.

Such harassments, the religious equivalents of the infamous
Star Chamber political proceedings of the same period, did not officially end until 1641, when the House of Commons banned ecclesiastical courts. While they lasted, England's New World colonies
came to be seen as places of physical and spiritual security for persecuted minorities. Some of these refugees even believed they were
reenacting the Exodus experience of the ancient Israelites who es-
caped Egyptian slavery; the Atlantic Ocean was a new Red Sea and
Anglican leaders in Britain were likened to the biblical Pharaoh.

But as so often happens, once the refugees were thousands of miles away from their tormentors, they instituted their own forms of oppression. The English colonists in North America may have likened their new home to the biblical land of milk and honey, but in reality it was often a land of prejudice, sour like vinegar rather than sweet like honey.

The American Colonies

The Puritans of the Massachusetts Bay Colony, the iconic pilgrims of Thanksgiving fame, were themselves intolerant of many other Christians. In 1636, for instance, about fifteen years after the first settlers arrived at Plymouth Rock, the colony's religious leaders expelled Roger Williams, a Baptist minister, from their midst. Williams had been teaching church-state separation, religious liberty (extending even to Catholics, Jews, and Muslims), and individual freedom of conscience — ideas that were not welcomed by the strait-laced Puritans. Here is how Williams described his view of interreligious relations in 1655:

> It hath fallen out sometimes, that both papists [that is, Catholics] and protestants, Jews and Turks [that is, Muslims], may be embarked on one ship; upon which supposal I affirm, that all the liberty of conscience, that ever I pleaded for, turns upon these two hinges — that none of the papists, protestants, Jews, or Turks, be forced to come to the ship's prayers of worship, nor compelled from their own particular prayers or worship, if they practice any.

This may seem like common sense today, but it was a radical idea in the Puritan colonies.

Meanwhile, English Quakers led by William Penn settled in Pennsylvania in 1682, and Anglicanism itself gained dominance in

Virginia following the establishment of Jamestown in 1607. Many of Georgia's first settlers were Baptists; when he arrived in 1733, James Oglethorpe envisioned the colony as a hospitable home for Britain's debtors and poor. Added to this mix were German and Scandinavian Lutherans, Dutch Calvinists, Scotch-Irish Presbyterians, as well as groups of English Methodists, Deists, Unitarians, Congregationalists, Catholics, and Jews.

When most Americans today, including Catholics and Jews, think of colonial America, they think of the story of the first Thanksgiving. Yet while this story paints a picture of mutual tolerance and understanding, the truth is that religious prejudice was an integral part of colonial America, including both anti-Catholic and anti-Jewish sentiment.

Optimism and pride about American history is to be commended when appropriate, but it cannot be allowed to cover the mirror of reality and distort the past.

It is true, for instance, that in 1632 Maryland was established as a colony that provided Catholics a safe haven. The English sovereign, Charles I, provided a charter to Lord Cecil Calvert, who had converted to Catholicism from Anglicanism in Britain. At the same time, however, no Catholics were permitted to live in Massachusetts, where in 1647 a law was enacted that threatened death to "all and every Jesuit, seminary priest, missionary or other spiritual or ecclesiastical person made or ordained by any authority, power, or jurisdiction, derived, challenged or presented, from the Pope or See of Rome." The Boston brewer and patriot Samuel Adams, whose cousin John would serve as the new nation's second president, declared over a century later, in 1768, "I did verily believe, as I do, still, that much more is to be dreaded from the growth of popery in America, than from the Stamp Act, or any other acts destructive of civil rights."

It was also difficult for Jews, who first arrived in the Dutch colony of New Amsterdam in 1654. There they faced the hostility of Governor Peter Stuyvesant, a staunch member of the Netherlands

Reformed Church. While some Jews were permitted to settle on Manhattan Island, they were faced with prejudice and anti-Jewish policies, which caused some to move to the more religiously hospitable colony of Rhode Island. In 1664 the British captured New Amsterdam and quickly changed its name to New York, ending Dutch rule on the continent but doing little to improve the situation of Jews there. When the Declaration of Independence was signed in Philadelphia, Pennsylvania, on July 4, 1776, all but one of the 56 signers was a white, Protestant male. The one exception, Charles Carroll of Maryland, was an advocate of full civil and political rights for Catholics, having once been banned from voting even in Maryland because of his religion.

The New Nation

Some revisionist historians today, particularly on the "Religious Right," posit the inaccurate thesis that America was founded as a "Christian nation." The nation's founders did indeed come from Christian backgrounds. Yet while they had every opportunity to make the new nation an officially Christian one, the primary source material and documents from the period indicate they consciously refused to do so. This was not a mistake or a result of carelessness. Rather, it was the result of a combination of history, demography, and a belief on the part of the founders that they were creating something unique in world history. The painful memory of religious persecution in England and in other parts of Europe, including the Spanish Inquisition, was still fresh in the collective memories of the founders. In addition, they were aware of the Thirty Years' War that took place on the European continent between 1618 and 1648: three decades of brutality in which Protestants and Catholics killed one another in great numbers — all, of course, in the name of God and faith.

The Declaration of Independence — hardly a carelessly written text — contains four specific religious references: "nature's God," "Creator," "Supreme Judge of the world," and "Divine Providence." None of these refers specifically to Jesus or Christianity. Likewise the conclusion of the United States Constitution, written in 1787, has a single bit of religious wording: "in the year of our Lord." While the Lord in question is certainly Jesus, this is a boilerplate phrase of dating that is still used today in some legal and ceremonial documents.

There is no constitutional authorization for the establishment of any religion in the United States; quite the opposite, in fact. Article Six states there can be no "religious test" for public office in the new republic, and the First Amendment, a part of the Bill of Rights, prohibits the establishment of religion while at the same time providing for the exercise of citizens' religious beliefs.

In addition to these historical and philosophical reasons, the founders had demographic reasons for not establishing any one church body as the official religion of the new nation. By 1776 the country was already religiously diverse, including many Protestant denominations, minority Catholic and Jewish populations, uniquely African expressions of Christianity practiced by enslaved populations, and the indigenous religions of Native Americans who were being systematically displaced. James Madison, the attorney and Presbyterian layman from Virginia who would become the nation's fourth president, predicted in *The Federalist Papers* that the new nation would be home to a "multiplicity of sects." He was not wrong.

Of course, some sects were more powerful than others. In 1790, the first national census revealed a population of fewer than four million people. It is estimated that at about this time the total Catholic population was about 25,000, or less than one percent of the national total, with about 15,000 in Maryland, 7,000 in Pennsylvania, 1,800 in New York, and the rest scattered in the other ten newly created states. Jews in the United States numbered about 3,000 in the same year.

Still, the issue of whether the U.S. would officially become a "Christian nation" complete with states collecting church taxes from their citizens remained in doubt until a legislative struggle took place in Virginia between two giants of American history, Thomas Jefferson and Patrick Henry. The scene of the 1785 battle was the state legislature in Richmond, while Henry was Virginia's first governor and fifteen years before Jefferson was elected U.S. president.

Henry, a member of Virginia's Anglican majority, wanted to impose a special tax on the state's residents, one that would support various religious institutions. Similar levies were imposed in many European nations. Because of Virginia's population at the time, most of the collected taxes would have gone to the dominant Anglican (or as it came to be called in the United States, Episcopal) Church. But Jefferson, who was raised in the Anglican tradition like Henry, was strongly opposed to the governor's proposal, and he enlisted both James Madison and Baptist minister John Leland as allies in a bitter but successful campaign to block the proposed bill. Madison wrote,

> The Episcopal clergy are generally for it. . . . The Presbyterians seem ready to set up an establishment which would take them in as they were to pull one down which shut them out. The Baptists, however, standing firm by their avowed principle of complete separation of church and state, declared it to be "repugnant to the spirit of the Gospel for the Legislation thus to proceed in matters of religion, that no human laws ought to be established for the purpose."

Thanks to the efforts of Jefferson and his allies, Henry's bill failed to be passed and in the following year the Virginia legislature adopted Jefferson's Statute of Religious Freedom by a vote of 74 to 20. It was an historic law that has had extraordinary influence upon American history for 225 years. It provided that no man shall be compelled to frequent or support any religious worship, place, or ministry whatsoever . . . nor shall otherwise suffer on account of his religious opinions or belief; but that all men shall be free to profess, and by argument to maintain, their opinion in matters of religion, and that the same shall in no wise diminish, enlarge, or affect their civil capacities.

Had Henry won the day with his church tax proposal, it is likely that the other newly independent American states would have followed Virginia's example and placed similar taxes on their citizens. Had that happened, America might have been far different from the nation we know today. Had Henry won, it would have been more difficult to write the federal Constitution two years later without the addition of specific religious language and perhaps the addition of an article approving a church tax or perhaps even mandating the establishment of a state religion. We can thank the Virginia legislature that this did not happen.

Letters from Washington and Jefferson

When George Washington, who also had an Anglican upbringing in Virginia, became president in 1789, the leaders of the Touro Synagogue, the Jewish congregation of Newport, Rhode Island, sent him a letter of congratulations. The synagogue building in Newport was dedicated in 1762 and is today a national historic site, the nation's oldest extant Jewish house of worship and the only structure of its type remaining from the colonial period. Washington responded to the warm greetings of the Newport Jewish community with a letter of his own that defined not only his view of religious liberty in America, but also reflected the thinking and beliefs of many of the nation's founders. Washington wrote:

Gentlemen:

While I received with much satisfaction your address replete with expressions of esteem, I rejoice in the opportunity of assuring you that I shall always retain grateful remembrance of the cordial welcome I experienced on my visit to Newport from all classes of citizens.

The reflection on the days of difficulty and danger which are past is rendered the more sweet from a consciousness that they are succeeded by days of uncommon prosperity and security.

If we have wisdom to make the best use of the advantages with which we are now favored, we cannot fail, under the just administration of a good government, to become a great and happy people.

The citizens of the United States of America have a right to applaud themselves for having given to mankind examples of an enlarged and liberal policy — a policy worthy of imitation. All possess alike liberty of conscience and immunities of citizenship.

It is now no more that toleration is spoken of as if it were the indulgence of one class of people that another enjoyed the exercise of their inherent natural rights, for, happily, the Government of the United States, which gives to bigotry no sanction, to persecution no assistance, requires only that they who live under its protection should demean themselves as good citizens in giving it on all occasions their effectual support.

It would be inconsistent with the frankness of my character not to avow that I am pleased with your favorable opinion of my administration and fervent wishes for my felicity.

May the children of the stock of Abraham who dwell in this land continue to merit and enjoy the good will of the other inhabitants — while every one shall sit in safety under his own vine and fig tree and there shall be none to make him afraid.

May the father of all mercies scatter light, and not darkness, upon our paths, and make us all in our several vocations useful here, and in His own due time and way everlastingly happy.

G. Washington

In 1802 Jefferson responded to a group of Baptists in Danbury, Connecticut, who, as a minority faith community in that state, asked the president about the status of religion and state in America. His written answer included the striking image of a "wall of separation" between church and state, an image that has endured and become part of the American legal and political lexicon for more than two centuries. Jefferson wrote:

Gentlemen

The affectionate sentiments of esteem and approbation which you are so good as to express towards me, on behalf of the Danbury Baptist association, give me the highest satisfaction. My duties dictate a faithful and zealous pursuit of the interests of my constituents, & in proportion as they are persuaded of my fidelity to those duties, the discharge of them becomes more and more pleasing.

Believing with you that religion is a matter which lies solely between Man & his God, that he owes account to none other for his faith or his worship, that the legitimate powers of government reach actions only, & not opinions, I contemplate with sovereign reverence that act of the whole American people which declared that their legislature should "make no law respecting an establishment of religion, or prohibiting the free exercise thereof," thus building a wall of separation between Church & State. (Congress thus inhibited from acts respecting religion, and the Executive authorised only to execute their acts, I have refrained from prescribing even those occasional performances of devotion, practiced indeed by the Executive of another nation as the legal head of its church, but subject here, as religious exercises only to the voluntary regulations and discipline of each respective sect.) Adhering to this expression of the supreme will of the nation in behalf of the rights of conscience, I shall see with sincere satisfaction the progress of those sentiments which tend to restore to man all his natural rights, convinced he has no natural right in opposition to his social duties.

I reciprocate your kind prayers for the protection & blessing of the common father and creator of man, and tender you for yourselves & your religious association assurances of my high respect & esteem.

Thomas Jefferson

Anti-Catholicism in America

Unfortunately, despite the language of the Declaration of Independence, the Constitution's guarantee of religious liberty, and the eloquent and powerful words of two of the nation's founders and first presidents, religious prejudice against Catholics and Jews continued and even intensified in the early years of the United States. An infamous law in Maryland, for instance, required all public officials to take the oath of office on a copy of the New Testament. This law, clearly anti-Jewish in intent, was not repealed until the 1820s, over half a century into the life of the new nation. Such anti-Jewish policies in the new nation were rooted in the traditional Christian prejudices against Jews, which we discussed in the last chapter. Indeed, many scholars believe that religious anti-Judaism is the source of economic, cultural, and political anti-Semitism of the kind that culminated in the mid-twentieth century with the genocide of the Nazi Holocaust.

The roots of anti-Catholicism in America are similarly easy to identify. They lie in the Protestant Reformation's demonization of the Catholic Church, especially its priests and nuns. The Reformers often described the Catholic Church as the "Whore of Babylon," a phrase from the New Testament book of Revelation, and the pope as the "Antichrist." Protestants perceived the Catholic Church as spiritually bankrupt — and, later, as a distinct threat in the struggle to gain dominance in the New World. In this sense, Britain's 1767 military defeat of the French in Canada about ten years before the American War of Independence was viewed not only as a triumph over a rival's colonial ambitions, but also as a Protestant victory over spiritually deficient Catholics.

Historian John Tracy Ellis has argued that "a universal anti-Catholic bias was brought to Jamestown in 1607 and vigorously cultivated in all the thirteen colonies from Massachusetts to Georgia." Catholics were legally barred from living in Anglican Virginia by a 1642 law that was soon imitated by Puritan Massachusetts. In other colonies Catholic clergy, especially those in the Jesuit order, were actively persecuted. Even Maryland, once a safe haven for Catholics, became a colony of the British Crown in 1689, when Protestants gained political control there. As a result, some Maryland Catholics moved to Pennsylvania, where the Quaker leadership permitted greater freedom of worship and conscience. Yet even Thomas Jefferson was suspicious of Catholics and their clergy:

> History, I believe, furnishes no example of a priest-ridden people maintaining a free civil government. . . . In every country and in every age, the priest has been hostile to liberty. He is always in alliance with the despot, abetting his abuses in return for protection to his own.

Things grew worse as the number of Catholic immigrants increased in the years before and after the American Civil War

(1861-1865). Many of the newcomers were from Ireland, whose relationship with Britain was long and conflicted. For instance in 1835 Lyman Beecher, a prominent Presbyterian preacher and president of Cincinnati's Lane Seminary, publicly advocated the exclusion of Catholics from any western settlements as Americans moved in increasing numbers beyond the eastern seaboard. Ironically, Beecher was the father of Harriet Beecher Stowe, who in 1852 published *Uncle Tom's Cabin,* the famous novel that drew enormous national attention to the evil of human slavery in the United States.

During much of the nineteenth century, Catholics were accused by nativist Americans, overwhelmingly Protestant, of undermining the American experiment in republican government. Sometimes these accusations were accompanied by violence. In 1842 a Catholic convent in Charlestown, Massachusetts, was set on fire; in 1844 a riot in Philadelphia resulted in the deaths of thirteen people and the destruction of two Catholic churches. When Bishop Francis Kenrick (1797-1863) of Baltimore, the most prominent Catholic theologian and biblical scholar of his time, objected to Catholic children using the King James Bible in the public schools, the American Protestant Association was formed to denounce the "principles of popery" because they were "subversive of civil and religious liberty."

Indeed, the question of education — and whether Catholic parents should be allowed to send their children to parochial schools — was a contentious one throughout the nineteenth century and well into the twentieth. Catholic clergy perceived the public school system of the time to be little more than a thinly veiled extension of Protestantism; in response, they developed a system of separate schools for Catholic children. Not surprisingly, many Protestants responded with hostility. In 1874, for instance, Senator James G. Blaine of Maine proposed a constitutional amendment that would have blocked any public money from being used to support parochial schools:

No money raised by taxation in any state for the support of
public schools, or derived from any public source, nor any
public lands devoted thereto, shall ever be under the control
of any religious sect, nor shall any money so raised or land so
devoted be divided between religious sects or denominations.

President Ulysses S. Grant supported the Blaine Amendment and
worried about a nation with "patriotism and intelligence on one
side and superstition, ambition, and greed on the other." Grant, a
Civil War hero, wanted public schools to be "unmixed with atheistic, pagan or sectarian teaching." This last of Grant's stated fears
was a not-so-subtle reference to Roman Catholicism.

While Blaine's amendment was never added to the Constitution, thirty-four states eventually adopted much of its language
and ideas. Even as late as 1924, the Oregon state legislature passed
a law requiring all students in the state to attend public schools.
The bill was declared unconstitutional, and in a harbinger of future collaborations between Catholics and Jews, the American
Jewish Committee, a civil rights and advocacy group established
in 1906, filed an amicus curiae brief with the U.S. Supreme Court,
defending the right of Catholic parents to send their children to
parochial schools. A bit later, the issue became a major flashpoint
between Cardinal Spellman and Eleanor Roosevelt, America's
first lady between 1933 and 1945.

Interestingly, despite, or perhaps because of, the widespread
anti-Catholic sentiment in the United States, much of the Catholic leadership in the U.S., especially the clergy, became strong
vocal supporters for all things American, in a public campaign
designed to demonstrate the loyalty of Catholics to the traditional American narrative, heritage, and culture. Less than a
century after the anti-Catholic activities of Blaine and Grant,
Cardinals Richard Cushing and Francis Spellman both espoused
a muscular and patriotic form of Americanism that would have
pleased both the senator and the president. A hundred years af-

ter Blaine offered his anti-Catholic constitutional amendment, John O'Connor, a career U.S. Navy chaplain, became the first Catholic selected as the senior chaplain at the U.S. Naval Academy in Annapolis, Charles Carroll's birthplace. The circle was complete.

The Catholic Experience in the Nineteenth and Twentieth Centuries

As the twentieth century began, many Catholics in America found themselves walking a political and theological tightrope. While nativist bigotry and prejudice made them feel like second-class citizens, the fear at the Vatican was that the Church's mostly immigrant flock would be assimilated into the Protestant mainstream. Many American Catholics emigrated from countries like Ireland, Poland, and Italy, where the Church dominated virtually every aspect of daily life. Coming to America required adjusting to a minority status in a country where Catholicism played only a minor role. During the era of large-scale Catholic immigration to the United States, the nation's pantheon of heroes and heroines contained few if any Catholics.

Nevertheless, as Catholic immigrants arrived *en masse* to an America that was already religiously defined, they also encountered an openness of both physical space and spirit that was lacking in their European Catholic homelands. In spite of prejudice and bigotry, Catholics in America found themselves accommodated, if not assimilated. As Catholics grew in population their influence expanded; in 1906 Boston, the historic epicenter of American Puritanism, elected its first Catholic mayor, John Francis Fitzgerald. "Honey Fitz," as he was called, went on to serve in the U.S. House of Representatives and was the father of Rose Kennedy and grandfather of John F. Kennedy. Meanwhile, many public service professions came to be dominated by Catholic immigrants:

teaching, law enforcement, public transportation, construction, and firefighting, to name a few.

As all this was happening, Catholics began to ask themselves and their leaders a vexing question: "Can I be both a faithful Catholic and an authentic American?" They understood that religion in the United States was voluntary, not legally mandated; in such a religiously "deregulated" context, the importance of individual freedom and private conscience became paramount. This was a major change for Catholics who came from nations where church and state were inextricably intertwined.

One response to this question is what James Carroll has called the "Americanist" impulse among Catholics — a love of American-style freedom, a buying into and internalization of the established (essentially Protestant) national narrative, and the adoption of a "live and let live" spirit with respect to religious diversity. Carroll argues that Americanist Catholics embraced religious pluralism, particularly in the form of full acceptance of and warm friendships with non-Catholic friends, neighbors, classmates, and business associates long before the Second Vatican Council was convened in 1962. A religious aspect, frequently unexpressed, of the "Americanist" position was the belief that people outside the Church also have the spiritual means to achieve religious salvation.

Such sentiments did not go unnoticed or unchallenged by the Vatican, of course. In 1899, when Spellman was ten years old and Cushing four, Pope Leo XIII denounced "Americanism" as a heresy in his Apostolic Letter *Testem Benevolentiae* ("Witness to our Good Will"). The pontiff warned Catholics of the dangers such a belief entailed, and while Leo's words reinforced Catholic traditionalism in the U.S., they did not settle the issue. The pope warned,

> The underlying principle of these new opinions is that, in order to more easily attract those who differ from her, the

Church should shape her teachings more in accord with the spirit of the age and relax some of her ancient severity and make some concessions to new opinions. Many think that these concessions should be made not only in regard to ways of living, but even in regard to doctrines which belong to the deposit of the faith. They contend that it would be opportune, in order to gain those who differ from us, to omit certain points of her teaching which are of lesser importance, and to tone down the meaning which the Church has always attached to them. . . . [W]e are not able to give approval to those views which, in their collective sense, are called by some "Americanism." But if by this name are to be understood certain endowments of mind which belong to the American people, just as other characteristics belong to various other nations, and if, moreover, by it is designated your political condition and the laws and customs by which you are governed, there is no reason to take exception to the name. But if this is to be so understood that the doctrines which have been adverted to above are not only indicated, but exalted, there can be no manner of doubt that our venerable brethren, the bishops of America, would be the first to repudiate and condemn it as being most injurious to themselves and to their country. For it would give rise to the suspicion that there are among you some who conceive and would have the Church in America to be different from what it is in the rest of the world.

In addition to religious pluralism and freedom of conscience, Carroll asserts that newly arrived Catholics were also confronted with American liberal democracy. That is, many of them were encountering for the first time a political process where their votes were equal to others — and because Catholics were overwhelmingly white, they did not face the same discrimination at the polls that African Americans suffered. Carroll writes:

43

Through the 19th century, for a variety of reasons, the Church was locked in struggle with many of the ideas associated with what would come to be called "liberal democracy," ideas well established in the political culture of the United States. Religious pluralism, the separation of church and state, freedom of the press, government based on natural rights — such notions were anathema in Rome, a way of thinking condemned by Pius IX in his 1864 "Syllabus of Errors." In 1899 when Leo XIII denounced as heresy what he called "Americanism" in his Apostolic Letter *Testem Benevolentiae,* it seemed the fulfillment of a long-simmering hostility.

Pope Leo's concern was [that] individual liberty . . . seemed to be taking root inside the Church. . . . But it was America's relativists such as William James and pragmatists such as John Dewey — more benign in their social designs than their European counterparts — who seemed especially threatening because, in the New World, ideas of social transformation came wrapped in claims to virtue, even piety.

. . . With their subversion of ecclesial hierarchy — suggesting also rejection of a hierarchy of truth — most Americans were seen by Rome to be practicing a sham Christianity, a prelude to secularism. And now, said Leo XIII, there were American Catholics who, like carriers of infection, wanted to bring this disorder into the Church and assume the "right to hold whatever opinions one pleases upon any subject."

Of course, while the Vatican was concerned about Catholics becoming too "American," most American Catholics in these years were more concerned about simply making a living in cities like Boston, New York, Pittsburgh, Detroit, Baltimore, St. Louis, Milwaukee, Cincinnati, Philadelphia, and Chicago. The 1893 depression increased unemployment and when the economic recovery came, it reached the immigrant communities last and least of all. "No Irish Need Apply" signs were a common sight in many American shops, stores, and factories, but an expanding American economy, especially in the early decades of the twentieth century, required more labor, more workers, more immigrants to stoke the furnaces of industry and to build the new infrastructures of cities (steel, subways, skyscrapers, ports, ships, roads, automobiles, tires, glass, trucks, railroad cars, and many other enterprises). In these years, the fathers of our three cardinals were Americanists all: Cushing's father, a blacksmith by trade, became an employee of the Boston transit system; Spellman's father was a successful entrepreneur grocer in Whitman, Massachusetts, before the age of chain supermarkets; and O'Connor's father was a bricklayer and an active trade union member.

Despite Pope Leo's condemnation of Americanism, the increasingly positive experience in the U.S. became a larger and larger factor in the lives of individual Catholics and their families — and among the Church hierarchy as well. It is not surprising that Cushing, Spellman, and O'Connor would give voice to the Americanist views of millions of American Catholics. Cushing's Americanism included a commitment to religious pluralism, which he acted on when he sought the excommunication of Leonard Feeney, an anti-Semitic and anti-Protestant Jesuit priest in Boston who publicly preached and taught what for centuries had been a basic belief for Catholics: *extra ecclesiam nulla sallus,* or "no salvation outside the Church." It also included a strong opposition to communism; for Cushing, communism was a real and present danger to the country he loved with such passion. Cushing also championed and supported the political aspirations of the Kennedy family, which eventually produced the first Catholic U.S. president, a reality that generations of earlier Americans, both Catholic and non-Catholic, could never have predicted or even imagined.

Spellman's Americanist beliefs fueled his impassioned and uncritical public support of the U.S. military. He was the prelate who, during the Korean War in the 1950s, called for more Catholic priests to enter the military chaplaincy — a request young John O'Connor heeded. At the zenith of his power as Archbishop of New York, Spellman traveled throughout the world to conduct religious services at overseas American military outposts during three wars (World War II, Korea, and Vietnam). He was even invited to be an official participant in closed strategy meetings at the Pentagon, where top secret military topics were discussed in his presence.

O'Connor's unique Americanist beliefs were put to the test in combat situations during the 1960s, when he served as a combat "padre" during the Vietnam War and later when he was chosen as the chief of chaplains of the U.S. Navy, a position that demanded supervision of Protestant clergy and rabbis as well as his fellow Catholic priests.

The reforms achieved at the Second Vatican Council — especially those having to do with religious liberty, ecumenism, and building positive relations with Jews — could never have happened without the support of a strong Americanist Catholic Church, one that was led at the time by Cardinal Cushing and Cardinal Spellman. By the time the twentieth century drew to a close, it appeared that Americanist ideas and ideals had triumphed within Catholicism, and that most vestiges of anti-Catholicism in America had been eradicated.

Presidents and Popes

One sign of the ebbing of anti-Catholicism was the growing number of meetings between popes and American presidents, a tradition that began in 1919 at the Vatican when President Woodrow Wilson, a Presbyterian minister's son, met with Benedict XV. But almost forty years passed before Dwight Eisenhower, a child of

Mennonite parents, met with John XXIII in 1959. After this such encounters increased in frequency, so that when Barack Obama met Benedict XVI in 2009 it was the twenty-seventh meeting in a series that has included five popes and twelve presidents. Included in this list is John Kennedy's single meeting with Paul VI in Rome in 1963; interestingly, J.F.K. was careful to only shake hands with the pope rather than kiss the pontiff's ring, which would be the usual etiquette for a Catholic.

Most of these meetings took place in Rome; only two pontiffs have set foot in the White House. When John Paul II visited the United States in 1979, Jimmy Carter, a Southern Baptist Sunday school teacher and former missionary, welcomed him there, in the first such papal visit in history. In 2008 George W. Bush, a born-again evangelical Protestant, received Benedict XVI in the White House. Although the two popes did not choose to do so, they could have easily unpacked their overnight luggage in the White House and been honored guests in the famous Lincoln Bedroom — something that would have been inconceivable in the days of Jefferson and Grant, and a far cry from the 1928 U.S. presidential campaign, when Alfred E. Smith's opponents were certain that if the Catholic governor of New York became president, the pope would effectively move into the White House and directly influence American political life.

Religious Pluralism

The term "cultural pluralism" was first coined by Horace M. Kallen, a rabbi's son, who taught for many years at several American colleges and universities. During the 1920s, he observed that the culture of the United States represents many values, beliefs, expressions, and facets. Kallen wrote that pluralism allows "for some degree of cultural diversity within the confines of a unified [American] national experience." He believed that every religious, ethnic, and racial group made significant contributions to the general society. Taken together, Kallen's concept of pluralism can be compared to the various threads of a lustrous tapestry reflecting the diversity that exists among the American people.

It did not take long for Kallen's concept to be adapted and applied to American religious life; certainly Cushing, Spellman, and O'Connor affirmed and acted on the concept of religious pluralism. Some compare cultural and religious pluralism to a symphony orchestra in which individual members each play different instruments. By themselves, they create only a basic melody or harmony, but playing together they have the potential to make beautiful music. Using this analogy, pluralism means that no individual or group of players is more dominant or important than any other.

But the reverse is also true. Pluralism can also result in a dissonant, discordant, and disruptive sound, with various orchestra members and instrumental groups competing with one another for prominence, dominance, or control. Many who are skeptical of religious pluralism believe that it undermines and weakens authentic religious beliefs. Others concede that theological diversity certainly exists, but that this is not necessarily a good thing, for in their hearts they are convinced that their own faith is superior to others.

In any case, pluralism, whether desired or not, means at least this: all religious groups have a distinctive contribution to make to the society and the right to spiritual self-definition. Pluralism, as Cushing, Spellman, and O'Connor understood the term, also means a religion with a large number of members is not superior to another religion that attracts a smaller number; size does not matter. A majority is not permitted to dominate or persecute a minority, as too often happens in religious as well as political life. Clearly, this kind of religious pluralism has not been accepted throughout the world, remaining a distant goal for many societies.

Our three American Catholic leaders were certainly aware

that their positive views about Jews and Judaism, and their acceptance of pluralism, were challenging and controversial, because religion, at its core, seeks to offer ultimate answers to questions about life and death, about human existence itself. For the cardinals, each in his way, to affirm that others, including Jews, have authentic answers to these basic questions was sometimes difficult for Catholic believers to accept.

Religious pluralism asserts there is a "multiplicity" (Madison's word from the eighteenth century) of authentic spiritual paths, and each path is legitimate for those who follow it. Too, people who affirm a different religious belief must be respected and protected from both verbal and physical assault and all other forms of discrimination. Cushing, Spellman, and O'Connor, of course, had no trouble celebrating and proclaiming the truth of their own religion, but they have gained a unique place in history because they were also able to acknowledge and recognize the truth of other religions, especially Judaism.

Indeed, any view of the extraordinary historic achievements of Cushing, Spellman, and O'Connor in transforming Catholic-Jewish relations and the Church itself will be incomplete without the backdrop of anti-Catholicism in the U.S., papal disapproval and mistrust of the "Americanist" influence on Catholics, and the negative reactions in the United States to the concept of religious pluralism. Overcoming these negative factors makes the successful efforts of the three cardinals even more remarkable.

While the great gains achieved by Cushing, Spellman, O'Connor and other pioneering Catholic leaders are applauded, there remains an intra-Catholic tension about the constantly evolving relationship between that ancient religious tradition and contemporary America. Consider two moments in the 1987 visit of Pope John Paul II to the United States. The pope held a successful, widely-reported meeting with American Jewish leaders in Miami, where he publicly declared "Never again!" in referring to the evils of the Holocaust. A few days later in a private meeting, he spoke to the country's bishops at the San Fernando Mission in Southern California. John Paul II was aware that some prelates in the U.S. spoke of "the American Catholic Church" and "American Catholics." However, according to reports at the time, the pope corrected such language by insisting there is only the universal Catholic Church in America with over 60 million members, and not an "American Church." The pope made clear that while there are many Catholics living in America, they are not "American Catholics."

Is the question of Catholic "Americanist" beliefs that was raised by Pope Leo XIII over a century ago completely settled? But then, is any major religious issue or question ever fully settled? Compared to the rest of the world, is our nation "America, the different"? Perhaps. Perhaps not. Who can say? In any case, it is clear that three very different Catholic leaders — Cushing, Spellman, and O'Connor — answered that question in the affirmative.

CHAPTER FOUR

J.F.K.'s Favorite Priest

———⟨∞⟩———

The Early Years

Richard James Cushing, the son of a blacksmith, was born on August 24, 1895, in south Boston. His parents, Patrick Cushing and Mary Dahill, were both Irish immigrants: Patrick, who arrived in the United States in 1880, was from County Cork, and his wife grew up in County Waterford. In Boston they resided at 808 East 3rd Street, in a house that was built in 1890.

From elementary school through seminary, all of Richard Cushing's education took place in Boston. Because there was no parochial school in his neighborhood, young Dickie Cushing attended the public Oliver Hazard Perry Grammar School on East 7th Street, located across from Boston Harbor. The three-story red brick Perry school building was opened in 1905 and Cushing was one of the first pupils to use the new facility. He graduated in 1908 in a class of 125 students, many of whom were also first-generation Irish-American Catholics. Boston at the time was a historic city, proud of its nickname "the Hub of the Universe," and a citadel of white, Anglo-Saxon, Protestant hegemony. Anti-immigrant feeling ran strong there, as it did in the nation as a whole, and Boston's newcomers, many of them Catholics and Jews, felt the sting of prejudice and discrimination.

South Boston High School was Cushing's next academic stop, but because he was either bored or suffering from what today would be diagnosed as a learning disability, the blacksmith's son accrued a sizable truancy record and dropped out of school before the end of his freshman year. Dropping out was fairly common in those days, and had Cushing continued down that path he might have taken a job as a day laborer on the Boston waterfront and eventually married one of the young Catholic women who worked as maids, nannies, or cooks in the homes of the Boston Protestant elite.

But the lad's parish priest, Father Mortimer E. Twomey of St. Eulalia's Church, saw something in the tall dropout with the angular face, who until then had shown little aptitude for academic inquiry or achievement. Twomey actively reached out to the young people in his parish by installing a two-lane bowling alley and a pool room in the church school building. And he hired Cushing to manage these facilities — a huge responsibility for a teenager beset with academic problems. The youth did well at his job, and years later he recalled that for him there were only two paths in his neighborhood: from the Cushing home to the church, and from the church back home. He soon became a general handyman in the parish: "I wasn't a pious lad. . . . I mowed lawns, stoked fires, shoveled snow, swept and mopped floors, opened the church in the morning and locked it up at night" after closing down the bowling alley and pool room.

Father Twomey, however, had higher hopes for his young protégé. He persistently urged Cushing to enroll at Boston College High School, the local Jesuit parochial academy. The youth obeyed, even taking a construction job to help pay the tuition of $60 per year (about $960 in 2010 dollars). But once he became an academy student, Cushing nearly drowned again in the turbulent waters of academic studies. He was tempted once again to drop out and take a job as a laborer, but Twomey and others came to his support. Finally, in June 1913, Richard Cushing graduated from

Boston College High School as a class officer, even speaking at the school's commencement ceremonies. And from there he matriculated at Boston College, where he studied for two years before taking the step that ultimately defined him and his life: in 1915 he entered Saint John's Seminary in nearby Brighton, where he studied for six years before he was ordained as a priest on May 26, 1921, along with twenty-six other men.

O'Connell and Cushing: Priests Apart

Officiating at that service was Cardinal William Henry O'Connell, the authoritarian archbishop of Boston from 1907 until his death in 1944 at age 84. No one at that ordination service could have guessed that fewer than twenty-five years later, Father Cushing would be O'Connell's successor. The newly ordained priest quickly returned to St. Eulalia's, where he celebrated his first Mass.

The leadership styles of O'Connell and Cushing make a revealing study in contrasts, helping to explain the love and esteem the latter man received from Boston Catholics. O'Connell was an imperious prelate who presided in regal style over the rapid increase in both the Catholic population and the Church's influence in the early years of the century. Under his autocratic rule, all things Catholic in Boston were under his tight personal control: parishes, hospitals, parochial schools, seminaries and colleges, orphanages, convents, monasteries, charities, and publications. Called "Number One" by both friends and foes, O'Connell was also at the center of several scandals, one of which involved nepotism to benefit his young nephew, James O'Connell, a priest who was later discovered to have secretly married and carried on a double life. Another focused on exactly how Archbishop O'Connell had accumulated his considerable personal wealth.

Unlike Cushing, O'Connell had no interest in pluralism; in

1908 he triumphantly summed up American history by saying that "the Puritan has passed. The Catholic remains." He opposed the Child Labor Amendment; he assessed Einstein's theories of relativity as "authentic atheism . . . camouflaged as cosmic pantheism." He encouraged his priests to withhold communion from women wearing lipstick, and in 1932 he condemned popular "crooners" of the era as pandering to "the basest appeal to sex emotion in the young." (No matter that two Catholics, Bing Crosby and Frank Sinatra, were soon to achieve worldwide fame as crooners.) Known for intimidating his priests, O'Connell once expressed particular contempt for one of his auxiliary bishops, Francis Spellman. "Francis," he remarked, "epitomizes what happens to a bookkeeper when you teach him to read." How dismaying for the 80-year-old Boston archbishop to see the "bookkeeper" made archbishop of New York in 1939!

When the haughty archbishop of Boston ordained Richard Cushing in 1921, it marked the end of a long, difficult road for the young cleric. The twenty-six-year-old Cushing was not particularly gifted theologically or rhetorically, but two other outstanding qualities enhanced his career: because of his personal struggles and working-class roots, he related warmly to people who lacked financial wealth, influential family connections, or exalted professional careers. In addition, the young Father Cushing was a superb fundraiser for Catholic charities and causes, a skill he had learned from Father Twomey.

But the same pattern of restlessness and need for change that had dogged Cushing as a student continued into the early years of his priesthood. In just two and a half months he served three parishes in the Roxbury and Somerville areas of metropolitan Boston, complaining to O'Connell that parish work was not the vineyard in which he wanted to labor. Reassigned to the South Boston office of the Society of the Propagation of the Faith, he finally began the work that prepared him for his future leadership roles, raising funds for Catholic missions around the world. While some of his contributors were wealthy, he was particularly effective at reaching out to people who made small donations. In the years before he became archbishop of Boston, his distinctive personality and raspy voice, with its unmistakable South Boston accent, would become known throughout his archdiocese.

Unlike parish priests who devote themselves to individual congregations, Cushing traveled throughout New England, speaking and raising money for the Society. He emphasized the importance of missions that provided academic and vocational education, medical care, and social welfare assistance as well as religious instruction. His unpretentious manner, "everyman" background, and obvious sincerity, especially in behalf of young children's needs — coupled with an inability to take "no" for an answer when requesting funds — drew the attention of archdiocesan officials, including O'Connell, who could not deny the achievements of the formerly unhappy young priest. And on June 29, 1939, Archbishop O'Connell — perhaps reluctantly, perhaps not — consecrated Cushing as a bishop in the Catholic Church.

Patrick Cushing, the new bishop's father, had died in 1922, but 81-year-old Mary Cushing was present for her son's ceremony in Boston's Cathedral of the Holy Cross. And in a curious quirk of history, so was Francis Spellman, the new archbishop of New York. A few years earlier, Spellman had returned to Boston after years of living in Rome. Having just been appointed to his new position, Spellman was attending the consecration as a kind of farewell gesture to Boston and his native Massachusetts. At the time, neither man could have known how their lives and careers would later intertwine, nor could they have known the extraordinary roles they were to play in shaping positive Catholic-Jewish relations a quarter century later.

Cushing's personal style, physical demeanor, and lack of rhetorical eloquence contrasted with the elegant Spellman, who was six years his senior. Spellman had studied theology in Rome, not Boston, and in 1916 he was ordained a priest at the Vatican, in 1932 becoming the first American to be consecrated a bishop in Rome in a ceremony presided over by the future Pope Pius XII. While Cushing connected to the common people in Boston, Spellman was connected to the centers of Vatican power.

In any case, as bishop Cushing continued his work as director of the Society for the Propagation of the Faith, and as an auxiliary bishop he often represented the aging Cardinal O'Connell, with whom he had a complex, ambivalent relationship that lasted until the older man's death in 1944. With a crusty countenance and a voice he once described as "similar to a fish peddler," Cushing found his intellect questioned by some. Yet others considered him "the salt of the earth" — the title, in fact, of an adoring biography written by John H. Fenton, New England bureau chief for the *New York Times.*

When Archbishop O'Connell died, the pope chose Cushing to take his place. The former high school truant and dropout, one-time indifferent student, and impatient young parish priest had reached the pinnacle of Catholic leadership in his native city. Many people expected that Cushing would receive the red hat of a cardinal at the Vatican — O'Connell was Boston's first cardinal — as soon as World War II ended and travel to Rome resumed. But this was not the case. Cushing had to wait fourteen years before he was appointed to the College of Cardinals — possibly due at least in part to the machinations of Francis Spellman. Spellman always had the ear of Pius XII, and some have speculated that the New York archbishop did not want his carefully crafted public standing as "America's Leading Catholic" threatened by a rival prince of the Church in historic Boston. Others have wondered whether Spellman wanted to punish Cushing for the way O'Connell, his predecessor, had showered contempt and derision upon him when he served as an underling in Boston.

But if Spellman and Cushing cut contrasting figures, Pope John XXIII and the Boston archbishop with the fish peddler's voice were simpatico. Things moved quickly after Pius XII died on October 9, 1958. Twenty-four days later Angelo Giuseppe Roncalli was the new pontiff, and twenty-four days after that the man whom Richard Cushing later called "Good Pope John" chose the south Boston native for membership in the College of Cardinals, which at that time had fewer than eighty members. (Today it has nearly 180).

The transition from O'Connell to Cushing as Boston archbishop meant more than just a change in personal styles. O'Connell, though born in Lowell, Massachusetts, in 1859, presided over a Church whose members were mostly newcomers to the United States. His task was to secure a public footing for his immigrant faith community, and during his forty-year tenure he succeeded in increasing the number of Catholic clergy, schools, parishes, and other tangible signs of a Church that was growing in power and size in Boston and elsewhere in New England. O'Connell made clear to both Catholics and non-Catholics that his Church, his people, and his community were in America to stay. He was openly disdainful of the Boston Protestant aristocracy, and his unofficial motto for Catholics could have been "Build, procreate, and expand."

An American or a Catholic?

Cushing became Archbishop of Boston on September 25, 1944, in a colorful ceremony in the Archdiocesan Cathedral on Washington Street. Although he may have seemed a surprising choice for the coveted leadership position, in many ways Cushing reflected the traditional religious upbringing of most Boston Catholics of his era, and above all and to the relief of many people, he was definitely *not* William Henry O'Connell. Yet Cushing's main task was different from his predecessor's. By 1944 the physical, political, social, and religious Catholic foundations in Boston were firmly in place. It was Archbishop Cushing's job to respond to a different need, namely, to develop an answer to a hostile question often hurled at Catholics: "Is it possible to be both an American and Catholic?" ("Is it possible to be both an American and a Jew?" was a question that was familiar to many Jews at the time as well.) Despite the size of the Boston Catholic population and the influence of such Catholic family dynasties as the Kennedys and the Fitzgeralds (the maternal branch of John Fitzgerald Kennedy's family), the legacy of anti-Catholicism remained a factor throughout Cushing's life.

In 1928 a Roman Catholic, New York State Governor Alfred E. Smith, was the unsuccessful Democratic candidate for president, running against Republican Herbert Hoover. His campaign gave rise to a series of anti-Catholic canards, centered on the question, *Can a Roman Catholic President faithfully follow the U.S. Constitution or will America's chief executive place Church laws and Vatican policies above everything else?* As cardinal, Cushing worked to inextricably link Catholicism with America, including the nation's history, its democratic institutions, church-state separation, religious liberty, and other historic values, customs, and ceremonies. To do so, he took a two-pronged approach, advocating anti-Communism as a sign of American nationalism, and positive interreligious relations as a sign of American inclusiveness. Such an approach refutes the conventional wisdom that a religious conservative must somehow be unable to develop positive relations with members of other faith communities — which is one reason why Cushing's historic achievements in Catholic-Jewish relations, both in Boston and at the Second Vatican Council, are so remarkable and so important to remember today.

Cushing was not unique as a Catholic in being a vigorous foe of Communism; during the 1948 Italian national elections, Pius XII threatened excommunication to Catholics who voted for Communist candidates. Yet Cushing's actions and oratory in this arena sometimes spilled over into right-wing extremism and American jingoism. In the 1950s he refused to publicly criticize U.S. Senator

Joseph McCarthy's campaign to root out Communism — the campaign that gave rise to the term "McCarthyism" to refer to demagoguery and the leveling of unsubstantiated accusations. In the 1960s he supported the ultra-conservative John Birch Society, an organization that once called President Dwight Eisenhower a "dedicated, conscious agent of the Communist conspiracy." His record also includes public support for Francisco Franco in Spain. Following the end of the Spanish Civil War in 1939, Cushing advocated trade with the Franco regime, a Fascist, anti-Communist government, closely allied with the Spanish Catholic Church, that had received military and political support from Nazi Germany in the late 1930s.

Cushing's anti-Communist speeches and rhetoric seem as strident today as when they were first uttered decades ago. In 1951 during the Korean War, Cushing struck a theme he reiterated many times:

> Love of God and love of country are linked together in the heart of every true Catholic American citizen. Patriotism, the noblest of the natural virtues, burns as brightly in the heart of the American Catholic as it does in the heart of any neighbor.... Yes, America, our country, we love thee, and we are ready, if necessary, to pour out the last drop of our blood in its defense.... We defy anyone to disprove the loyalty of the Catholics of the United States, to the government under which we live.

Eight years later, he addressed the Catholic Daughters of America and assailed Communism:

> Communism is a three-fold disease. It is a disease of the body because it kills; a disease of the mind, because it is associated with systematized delusions not susceptible to rational argument; and a disease of the spirit because it denies

God, materializes man, robs him of spirit and soul and reduces him to a level of the beast of the field.

During the 1950s and into the 1960s Cushing was the patron of the Oriel Society, based in Flushing, New York. The Society was a lay-led Catholic group dedicated to converting former Communists to Catholicism. The best known of these was Louis Budenz, who was born in 1891 to an Indianapolis Catholic family but joined the U.S. Communist Party in the 1930s, eventually serving as managing editor of the Communist newspaper the *Daily Worker.* He was also a spy for the Soviet Union. But in 1945 Budenz left the Party and at Saint Patrick's Church in New York City returned to the Catholic Church. Cushing called Budenz an "exemplary citizen of the City of God and the City of Man." Today Budenz is best remembered as an "expert" witness on the inner workings of the U.S. Communist Party, a former Party member who offered extensive though dubious and questionable Congressional testimony and who worked closely with the Federal Bureau of Investigation in identifying alleged Communists within the American government.

During the height of McCarthy's anti-Communist campaign, the influential Catholic journals *America* and *Commonweal* condemned the senator, as did some priests, including the social activist Monsignor George G. Higgins. When Cushing was asked about McCarthy's tactics that supposedly exposed active Communists within the U.S. Government, Cushing responded,

> I sympathize with anyone interested in keeping Communism in all its phases and forms from uprooting our traditions and our wonderful opportunity of assuming leadership throughout the world that is the only hope of oppressed people.

Cushing's initial support for the John Birch Society was clear in a response he wrote on April 20, 1960, when questioned about the right-wing organization:

> Replying to your letter, I beg to advise you that I do not know of any more dedicated anti-Communist in this country than Robert Welch [a founder of the John Birch Society]. I unhesitatingly recommend him to you and endorse his John Birch Society.

In perhaps his strongest statement on the subject, two years after John Kennedy was elected U.S. President, Cushing crowned his anti-Communist attacks by asserting: "Communism is the greatest enemy the Catholic Church has had to face in its 1,962 years of its existence."

But Cushing had his limits. Four years later, he appeared on a Boston radio program and struck a far different tone about the extremist Society, which had recently labeled as Communists not only President Eisenhower, but also Franklin Roosevelt and John F. Kennedy. This was too much for the irate cardinal, who fired back,

> I never met President Roosevelt. I am proud to add, however, that I knew the late President Kennedy better than any member of the John Birch Society and all of them put together.
>
> If it is true that two members of this society called my nearest and dearest friend, the late John F. Kennedy, a Communist, they and their associates owe the people of all nations who loved him and who will never forget his tragic death, an apology.
>
> If it is also true that two members of the Birch Society identified me with such an incredible remark, I cannot dignify them with an answer save to say — shame, shame, shame for attempting to blight the character and mar the memory of a martyr to his country with that of a traitor.

While Cushing's anti-Communism remained with him to the end of his life, his rhetoric cooled as a result of three events in 1961:

President Kennedy's meeting with Soviet Premier Nikita Khrushchev in Vienna; the failed Bay of Pigs invasion of Fidel Castro's Cuba, for which J.F.K. took full responsibility; and John XXIII's papal encyclical *Mater et Magistra,* which was directed more against colonialism than communism. At about the same time, the Vatican's public opposition to war in general was emphasized by Pope Paul VI in his 1963 address to the United Nations. By the mid-1960s many American Catholics in Boston and throughout the U.S. had shifted away from the kind of lockstep opposition to Communism that Cushing had been articulating for decades. It may be that he began taking more cues from the Kennedys, to whom he was a close friend and spiritual advisor, as well as from the post-Pius XII Vatican.

The 1960 Presidential Election

The cardinal's delicate minuet with the 1960 J.F.K. presidential campaign offers a study in both Cushing's Irish Catholic pride and his political sophistication. It offers a preview of how and why Cushing was able, four years later, to play a decisive role in guaranteeing the adoption of a positive declaration on Jews and Judaism at the Second Vatican Council. Essentially, Cushing believed that attacks on Kennedy's fitness for the White House based on his Catholicism were an insult to the higher principles of America, just as he believed that any form of anti-Semitism on the part of Catholics insulted the higher principles of Catholicism. While extremely careful not to specifically endorse J.F.K. for president, Cushing attacked anti-Catholic rhetoric and made known his opposition to anyone who opposed Kennedy on solely religious grounds.

Yet given his long, deep connection to the Kennedys, it was no accident or surprise that he supported J.F.K. for president. Cardinal O'Connell had officiated at the wedding of Joseph P. Kennedy and Rose Fitzgerald in 1915, but Cushing performed the marriage ceremony of John F. Kennedy and Jacqueline Bouvier. In the ensuing years he christened the couple's children and offered a prayer at J.F.K.'s inauguration in 1961, where he was joined by Rabbi Nelson Glueck, the president of Hebrew Union College-Jewish Institute of Religion; Archbishop Iakovos of the Greek Orthodox Church of North and South America; and the Rev. Dr. John Barclay, pastor of the Central Christian Church in Austin, Texas, and a reminder of the presence on the ticket of Lyndon B. Johnson of the Lone Star State.

A close reading of Cushing's prayer that day provides deeper insight about his political views than about his theological beliefs. The word "responsibilities" appears nine times, and "cooperation" four. It focuses on humanity's need to work together to solve the world's many problems in "these troubled but hopeful times." It implores Americans to "revere in every man that divine spark which makes him our brother," and to "defend my right to be myself; to defend my neighbor's right to be himself and to defend America's duty to respect the rights of all men." There is only a passing reference in the prayer to Cushing's anti-Communist passion: his fellow Americans, as "free men," are "to perform with complete vigilance our duty to prevent the spread of totalitarian terrorism everywhere."

Cushing's 1961 presidential prayer indicates some of the reforms that were adopted a few years later during the Second Vatican Council. The reforms include freedom of conscience, religious liberty, and positive interreligious relations with non-Catholics, especially Jews. By 1961 these ideas and beliefs were already an integral part of Cushing's thinking and public speech. (An historical/linguistic note: on Inauguration Day 1961, Cushing did not recite a single Latin phrase from his Church's liturgy, nor did Iakovos utter any Greek in his invocation, and Barclay used only English. It was left to Glueck to employ Hebrew, one of the three Western classical languages along with Latin and Greek. The rabbi closed his prayer with the original Hebrew words of the famous three-fold Priestly Benediction found in the Torah in Leviticus 12.)

Just a few years later, in 1963, the Kennedy family chose Cushing to officiate at the assassinated president's funeral in Washington's St. Matthew's Cathedral and his burial in Arlington National Cemetery. Anyone who lived through those painful days will always remember the somber image and gravelly voice of the cardinal. In the years to come Cushing remained a pastor to the Kennedy family, especially the president's widow. Just before Christmas Day 1965, Jacqueline wrote a brief note to the cardinal:

> I was so deeply touched to read your letter of December 10th and I can't tell you how much it means to me . . . to know that Jack continues to be remembered by the religious community in all parts of the world.
>
> You have done so much to keep his memory alive. . . .
>
> *Respectfully, Jackie*

Excommunicating an Anti-Semitic Priest

By the 1960s, Cushing had absorbed the concept of American pluralism and made it his own, albeit with some Catholic variations. In addition to whatever influence the Kennedys may have exercised, two events in his personal and professional life also helped pave the way for his strong positive action at the Second Vatican Council: his sister's long, successful marriage to Richard Pearlstein, a member of Boston's Jewish community, and the excommunication of Father Leonard Feeney, an ultraconservative anti-Semitic priest in Boston. Both these experiences decisively shaped his thinking about Jews and Judaism.

Leonard Feeney was a Jesuit priest who championed ultra-traditional Catholic positions; the signature belief of Feeney and his followers was the stance that salvation was impossible outside the Church. Following World War II, Feeney directed St. Benedict's Educational Center in Cambridge, Massachusetts, near Harvard University. The Center was established in 1942 by Catholic students as part of Boston College, and in addition to offering credit courses on Catholic subjects it actively sought to convert non-Catholics to the faith. When Feeney became its director in 1949, its orientation became more and more conservative, to the point that members of its faculty accused Boston College's president, a Catholic priest, of heresy for permitting the college's students to believe that other Christian churches could bring believers to salvation.

Four days after this charge was levied, Cushing came down hard on Feeney and his allies at the Center in a public statement that hinted strongly at his commitment to ecumenism:

> The so-called "St. Benedict Centre" is henceforth totally without ecclesiastical approbation, and attendance at it is strictly forbidden to Catholics. . . . [*Father*] Feeney, because of grave offenses against the general laws of the Catholic Church, has lost the right to perform any priestly functions, including preaching and teaching of religion.

Unsurprisingly, a rebellious Feeney kept his Center open and remained defiant by asserting repeatedly there was no salvation outside the Catholic Church. In October 1949 Feeney was excommunicated from the Church and dismissed from the Jesuit order. In time he and his followers, the "Feeneyites," began to march and demonstrate on the Boston Commons, where they publicly denounced Protestants, Jews, and Masons. In the years to come they would protest everything from the presence of Protestants on the University of Notre Dame football team to the construction of Protestant, Jewish, and Catholic chapels on the campus of the Jewish-sponsored Brandeis University.

Feeney's vicious anti-Semitism would have disturbed Cushing in any case, but it was especially painful because of his love for his Jewish brother-in-law. There is little doubt his relationship with Richard Pearlstein played an important role in moving Cushing toward Feeney's excommunication. If God loved Dolly, as Cushing believed, and Dolly loved Richard, then God must also love his beloved sister's husband, his people, and their religion. Speaking to a group of Episcopal priests in February 1964, Cushing said,

> We must not quarrel over them [differences in religious beliefs]. . . . We are told there is no salvation outside the Church — nonsense! Nobody can tell me that Christ died on Calvary for any select group! . . . As the feller says, "It is great to live with the Saints in Heaven, but it's hell to live with them on earth!"

Everyone in the audience knew exactly who the cardinal had in mind with that remark. By 1962 when the Second Vatican Council began its work, Cushing was a well-known religious leader whose style, actions, and policies made him a "different" cardinal for millions of non-Catholic Americans. Yet until he made his powerful speech in Rome urging a profound change in how the Church and its members viewed Jews and Judaism, Cushing was erroneously perceived, even by his admirers, as simply a warm pastor with limited intellectual skills.

Yet just seven months after speaking to that group of Episcopal priests, Cardinal Richard Cushing would dramatically and permanently transform Christian-Jewish relations at the Second Vatican Council. As we have seen, much of his entire life and career was preparation for his historic moment in St. Peter's Basilica in Rome, where he delivered the most important speech of his life.

The once indifferent student, the restless priest, the man who never liked to leave his beloved Boston, traveled to Rome where he would both change and make history.

CHAPTER FIVE

"The American Pope" Stands and Delivers

—◦◦◦—

The Early Years

No one was ever neutral about Cardinal Francis Joseph Spellman. During his lifetime, it seemed everyone had an opinion of the man who as archbishop of New York from 1939 until 1967 was a major player on the global religious and political stage. Indeed, even today, over forty years since his death, he continues to stir controversy.

An alphabetical list of the ways in which he was perceived by his flock, family, friends, and foes, might look something like this: ambitious, brutal, charming, dedicated, energetic, faithful, gifted, hateful, imperious, jealous, kingly, loyal, manipulative, nuanced, opulent, patriotic, quarrelsome, respected, successful, tyrannical, unwavering, virtuous, warlike, xenophobic, Yankee, and zealous. Yet this is just a beginning; another twenty-six positive and negative descriptions could easily be added, and probably twenty-six more after that. This is because during the middle decades of the twentieth century, Spellman rivaled the American president and the pope in terms of raw power and influence in religion, culture, and both domestic and international politics.

To better understand this man, let us begin by looking at his early life, family, and education, all of which formed a background that differed sharply from that of his contemporary, Cardinal Richard Cushing, and from that of Cardinal John O'Connor, who served as New York's archbishop a generation later. Spellman's father and mother were both born in the United States; their parents emigrated from Ireland in the mid-nineteenth century. Thus Spellman always considered himself more American than Irish. William Spellman, the future cardinal's father, was born in Whitman, Massachusetts, in 1858, and in 1888, at the "advanced" age of 30, he married Ellen Conway, two years his junior and also a Massachusetts native. Francis Joseph, born on May 4 of the following year, was the first of the couple's five children.

William Spellman initially worked in the small town of Whitman's shoemaking industry, but eventually became a successful grocer, purchasing a large home for his family on a five-acre lot. Because the largely Protestant Whitman had no Catholic schools, Francis graduated from the town's public high school in 1907; out of a class of 22, he was one of eight to pursue a college education. Over the course of his school years he served as an altar boy, was a first baseman on Whitman High's baseball team despite being only five feet five inches tall, and developed an interest in photography. In later years this hobby became an asset, as he ascended the ladder of clerical success. Taking photographs of various teachers, mentors, and members of the Church hierarchy and then presenting the portraits as gifts made many friends in high places for the ambitious Spellman.

In spite of being a child of Irish Catholic immigrants, Spellman's father assimilated many of the Protestant Yankee traits of New England and transmitted them to his eldest son: hard work, financial frugality, self-discipline, prudence, and patience. One of William's wry aphorisms stayed with Francis all his life: "Son, always associate with people smarter than yourself, and you will have no difficulty finding them." One night when an excited Francis came home from college and announced to his parents he had won an academic award, William's immediate reply was, "Did you put out the light downstairs?" But William Spellman was a distant, often aloof parent, and young Francis was always closer to his more approachable mother.

In 1907 Spellman permanently left Whitman to enroll at Fordham College (now University), which at the time was a small Jesuit school in the Bronx with only 105 students. His four years there passed uneventfully: he switched from baseball to tennis, and he improved his photography skills. And he decided to enter the priesthood. It was his graduation day when he told his parents of his decision; Ellen was thrilled, but William, always the cautious "Catholic Yankee," wanted assurance that his son was firm in his choice of a religious vocation.

In 1911 there was no indication that Francis Spellman was destined to become a prince of his Church, not just a close friend to Pope Pius XII but a viable candidate to succeed him. At age 22 Spellman had been a good student but not someone who exhibited exceptional intellectual or theological capacities. It seemed likely he would return to Massachusetts and enter seminary in Boston, a city that was rapidly increasing in Catholic population, institutions, and prestige. Instead, though, the young man boldly sought the permission of his clerical superior, Archbishop William O'Connell of Boston, to study at the prestigious Pontifical North American College in Rome. Sometimes called the "American Catholic West Point," the North American College was established in 1859 as an institution for the most promising young seminarians from the United States.

O'Connell himself had studied there, and he gave Spellman permission to do so as well. Spellman's solidly middle-class family provided the necessary funds to accompany the archbishop's ecclesiastical endorsement, and in the autumn of 1911 he boarded a ship for Europe, where he spent the next five years, far away from the life he had previously known. Looking back a century later, we can only speculate as to what motivated Spellman to eschew the usual path to the priesthood that most American men followed. Was he consciously or unconsciously emulating his superior? We will never know, but one thing is certain: during his years in Rome Spellman honed his skill in cultivating friendships with influential individuals. The NAC administration and faculty were not overly impressed with Frank Spellman's academic abilities. But he possessed superior administrative skills, an excellent memory for names, and the previously mentioned camera, and many of the friendships he made in Rome lasted a lifetime. In particular Spellman sought out the friendship of three Italian priests, all of whom became important cardinals: Gaetano Bisleti (1856-1937), the Vatican official in charge of Catholic education; Francesco Borgongini-Duca (1884-1954), the apostolic nuncio (that is, the Vatican's ambassador) to Italy during the tumultuous years from 1929 to 1953; and, the most powerful of the three high churchmen, Domenico Tardini (1888-1961), who served as Pope John XXIII's secretary of state (in essence the Vatican's prime minister).

The Art of Romanita

Spellman quickly became an expert in *Romanita,* the term used to describe the art of subtly bestowing personal favors to cement friendships. Such friendships were then converted into influence for the individuals who had provided the favors. At the apex of his fame and authority, Spellman practiced *Romanita* better than anyone else within the global Catholic Church. Years later, that talent earned him many friends in high places — the Vatican, the White House, the United States Congress, the New York City Hall, the Federal Bureau of Investigation, the media, and the Pentagon. Of course, it usually happens that when an ambitious young man seeks the favor of older teachers and mentors, he attracts both negative and positive responses. Spellman's Roman friends, both clergy and laity, were flattered and pleased by the young American's attention and largesse, but O'Connell, his ecclesiastical superior in Boston, had a far different opinion, calling the Roman-trained priest from Whitman a "little popinjay."

Although he often spoke with pride of his "Americanism," in reality Spellman was permanently "Vaticanized" during his years in Rome. That is, he recognized that the true source of his power in the church would never stem from his actions and pastoral work in the United States. Rather, it would always be connected to the Holy See and its leaders, especially Eugenio Pacelli, the man who became Pope Pius XII. The Vatican always remained Spellman's theological and professional lodestar.

On May 14, 1916, in the midst of World War I, Francis Spellman was ordained a priest by Archbishop Giuseppe Ceppetelli, the same man who had ordained the future Pope John XXIII, Angelo Giuseppe Roncalli, a dozen years earlier. Yet if Father Spellman expected a warm welcome and an important position upon his return to Boston, he must have been disappointed. O'Connell first dispatched the newly ordained priest to serve as pastor in a home for elderly Catholic women. A short time later Spellman became a church curate in the Roxbury neighborhood of Boston, where his multiple responsibilities included supervision of the parish school, visiting the ill, teaching the First Communion and Confirmation classes, Sunday preaching, and coaching the church's baseball team — a departure from his heady student days in Rome when he was frequently in the company of cardinals.

As a patriotic American, and perhaps as a priest eager to escape the oppressive O'Connell, Spellman volunteered to serve as a military chaplain in World War I. But the U.S. Navy rejected him because of his short stature and poor eyesight. One of the government officials who turned down Spellman's request for active duty was Franklin D. Roosevelt, the Assistant Secretary of the Navy, a 35-year-old Episcopalian from Hyde Park, New York, who three years later would be the Democratic Party's vice-presidential nominee and in 1932 would win the presidency. In an ironic twist of history, less than twenty years later Spellman would become a confidant of President Roosevelt, in a complex relationship that only ended with F.D.R.'s death in 1945. And in December 1939 Spellman, already the Archbishop of New York, became the Apostolic Vicar for the U.S. Armed Forces, a position that put him in charge of all Catholic chaplains in the U.S. military. In that role he traveled all over the world to conduct religious services for U.S. military personnel.

In 1917 the Army accepted Spellman's request for chaplaincy duty, but O'Connell vetoed the idea, moving Spellman to yet another menial assignment: four-and-a-half years of selling subscriptions to the *Pilot,* the archdiocesan newspaper. His dedication and diligence even in such a low-level job seemed about to bring him in from the cold. In 1924, he was appointed a chancery assistant in the archdiocesan headquarters. But O'Connell struck again, this time assigning Father Frank to the position of archdiocesan archivist, with an office in the basement of the chancery building. It may have been intended as a professional exile, but it enabled Spellman to gain knowledge of almost everything and everyone in the Boston archdiocese, including the archbishop himself, even as he remained outwardly loyal and obedient. The young priest curbed any visible anger and performed his assigned tasks with skill and talent; he was, after all, the son of a stoic Yankee Catholic.

But with time on his hands in the chancery basement, Spellman devised a strategy to free himself from the drudgery that O'Connell had imposed upon him. He translated two theological books by Francesco Borgongini-Duca into English, an act the Vatican cardinal deeply appreciated. Soon the wheels of *Romanita* began to turn, and in 1925 Spellman became the first American ever appointed to serve within the prestigious Vatican Secretariat of State. It was a promotion O'Connell could neither prevent nor block. The biblical children of Israel suffered in the wilderness for forty years before entering the Promised Land;

Spellman's wilderness experience under O'Connell was now over after far less time. The priest/photographer/archivist/translator/ newspaper salesman was back in the exact place he wanted to be: the corridors of power at the Holy See in Rome.

Return to Rome

Spellman was warmly received in the Vatican; Borgongini-Duca personally greeted him at the Rome railroad station upon his arrival from the U.S. Happily liberated from the chancery basement, Spellman was soon serving as translator, tour guide, and spiritual advisor to important American visitors to the Vatican — in essence, the Vatican's go-to man in anything and everything involving the United States. Among those important visitors in the 1920s were Nicholas Brady and his wife Genevieve. Brady was a wealthy captain of industry whose vast holdings included electric, gas, and mining companies, all anchored in his family's financial firm. Brady's company provided the funds for Walter P. Chrysler to begin an automobile company, and Brady himself served on Chrysler's board of directors. Born an Episcopalian, Brady was a convert to Catholicism, and he and his wife were considered the leading lay Catholics in America, perhaps in the entire world at the time. The couple was eager to be part of the glittering social and religious scene at the Vatican, and Spellman made certain that they were included in the Holy See's A-list of invited guests. Over the years the Bradys became major supporters of Catholic charities, and in return they were awarded the honorific titles of papal duke and duchess. In his turn, Brady provided Spellman with a Chrysler limousine as a gift for Cardinal Pietro Gasparri, in the Spellman hallmark of *Romanita*.

In 1927 Spellman first met Eugenio Pacelli, the Vatican nuncio, or ambassador, to Germany, who twelve years later would become Pope Pius XII. For Spellman, it was the most important personal encounter and the deepest friendship of his entire life. It was Pacelli who expedited Spellman's climb up the hierarchical ladder. Thus, in 1932 Spellman became the first American in history to be consecrated as bishop at the Vatican, donning the same vestments Pacelli had worn when the future pope became a bishop a decade earlier. Soon after becoming pope, Pacelli appointed Spellman archbishop of New York, and later presided at the ceremony in which he was officially made a member of the College of Cardinals.

While the two men were sufficiently close that they often vacationed together in various European destinations, on the face of it theirs was a strange relationship: Spellman, the short, rotund Massachusetts Yankee from a heavily Protestant community; and Pacelli, the tall aristocrat with deep family roots in Roman society. Pacelli was aloof, emotional, ascetic in appearance, and impatient, while Spellman was self-controlled and informal, and, as he had shown in his Boston years of priestly servitude under O'Connell, he was also enormously patient. Yet Pacelli respected Spellman's skill at mastering, indeed conquering the multilayered Vatican bureaucracy, while Spellman admired Pacelli's intellect and correctly sensed that the Italian cardinal, thirteen years older than himself, would someday reach the height of Church leadership. As it turned out, neither man was wrong in his assessment of the other.

Because of his many contacts in the business and financial worlds, Spellman was able to raise urgently needed funds for the Vatican when he was New York's archbishop, and he provided Pius XII with important insights into the intricacies of American political and religious life. Spellman became the human bridge between Franklin Roosevelt's White House and Pius XII's Vatican. The pope always made it clear that Spellman was his favorite and most important cardinal in the United States, and Spellman was able to call Pius XII directly on the trans-Atlantic telephone, something no one else in the American Catholic hierarchy was permitted to do. During Spellman's many visits to Rome in the years following World War II, he always lunched privately with the pontiff, a rare privilege.

Of course, Spellman's life in the Vatican was not exclusively about making social connections. In 1931, a year before he became a bishop, he was asked by Pius XI to hand-deliver a personal copy of the anti-Fascist encyclical *Non Abbiano Bisogno* ("We do not need") to the press corps in Paris; it was an encyclical that Benito Mussolini, the Fascist dictator of Italy, did not want made public. Spellman undertook the dangerous task and successfully presented the encyclical to media representatives in the French capital. Not surprisingly, his personal standing at the Vatican rose even higher after the conclusion of this risky mission in behalf of the pope.

Back to America — and Beyond

After this, for the second and last time in his life Spellman returned to Boston after a lengthy stay in Rome. Unsurprisingly, he received a cold welcome from now-Cardinal O'Connell, and indeed relations between the two men grew so strained that O'Connell did not attend the funeral of Spellman's mother in 1935. Spellman became the pastor of a church in Newton Centre, though in typical fashion he was patient, resolute, and managed to avoid being confined. Cardinal Pacelli had become the Vatican secretary of state in 1930 and was the clear heir apparent to the papal throne. In the autumn of 1936 he made a well-publicized visit to the United States that covered 8,000 miles, making public appearances in Washington, Los Angeles, San Francisco, Cleveland, Philadelphia, New York, and Chicago. Spellman, of course, was his escort and constant companion. The American press and general public were enthralled with the aristocratic Pacelli, but Spellman made certain that the press was not able to ask Pacelli a single question, even after a meeting with President Roosevelt at F.D.R.'s home in Hyde Park, New York.

The *New York Times* reported that the visiting cardinal had a threefold agenda: he wanted the U.S. to become active in the fight against Communism, especially since the Roosevelt administration had diplomatically recognized the Soviet Union in 1933. He also wanted Washington to send an official ambassador to the Vatican. Finally, he wanted to make clear to the president that the Vatican did not support or encourage the anti-Semitic, anti–New Deal views of Father Charles Coughlin of Detroit, whose popular weekly radio program reached millions of Americans.

The always charming but canny Roosevelt did not deliver on the first two items. While he was clearly anti-Communist, in 1936 F.D.R. was more concerned about the growing menace of Hitler's Nazism and he perceived the Soviet Union as part of a necessary anti-Nazi coalition. The president did appoint a "personal envoy" to the Vatican, but an exchange of ambassadors between the Holy See and Washington did not take place until the 1980s, during the Reagan administration. Yet in return for the cold porridge offered by the president, Pacelli began the process of silencing the bigoted Coughlin.

One casualty of the Pacelli visit was the relationship between Spellman and Genevieve Brady. The duchess's first husband had died six years earlier, but she had subsequently married William J. Babington Macaulay, Ireland's envoy to the Vatican, which allowed her to maintain her coveted contacts in Rome. She also retained use of the large Brady estate on Long Island, even though she had donated it to the Jesuits following her husband's death. (Today it is a Catholic retreat center.) Spellman had promised her that Cardinal Pacelli would be her guest there, but the whirlwind schedule he devised ultimately made that impossible. A furious and insulted duchess did host an elegant dinner in Pacelli's honor at her estate, but she was never close with Spellman again; he was not surprised to learn when she died two years later that she had cut him out of her will.

A Winning Trifecta

Yet while he lost her friendship, through Pacelli's visit he won a trifecta: he drew even closer to the future pope, solidified his relationship with F. D. R., and became a confidant of Joseph Kennedy. No shabby achievement for an auxiliary bishop from Boston still chafing under his superior's heavy hand. And indeed, Spellman was soon to be out from under that hand: when Pacelli won 61 of 62 votes cast by the College of Cardinals to elect a new pope in 1939 (modesty prevented him from casting a vote for himself), he quickly chose Spellman to succeed Cardinal Patrick Hayes of New York. Despite O'Connell's decades-long campaign of hostility, Spellman had finally outmaneuvered him and gained the top Catholic position in America. The former high school first baseman from Whitman soon became known as the "American Pope," not just because of his status, but because of his aggressive, forceful personality, his well-publicized alliance with Pius XII, and his fiery anti-Communism and pro-Americanism. Like Richard Cushing, Spellman supported Franco's Fascists during the Spanish Civil War in the 1930s, the divisive anti-Communist campaign of Senator Joseph McCarthy in the 1950s, and American military involvement in Vietnam in the 1960s. He was also a fervent but unsuccessful advocate of gaining public money for Catholic parochial schools.

The shrewd Spellman continued to accumulate friends in high places, both religious and political — not just F.D.R. and Joseph Kennedy, but also British prime minister Winston Churchill, F.B.I. director J. Edgar Hoover, New York State governor Nelson Rockefeller, and many others who were indebted to Spellman for a variety of political and personal reasons: it was *Romanita* practiced on a grand scale. For instance, in 1962 when Rockefeller, a Protestant, divorced his first wife to marry another woman, who had given up custody of her four children to gain her own divorce, much of the New York State Protestant leadership assailed the governor for his actions. But Spellman publicly defended Rockefeller when he remarried the following year. And since Rockefeller depended on the cardinal's support for his ultimately unsuccessful bid for the Republican presidential nomination two years later, Spellman gained an important ally in his continuing quest to secure state funds for parochial schools.

Spellman was not friends with everyone, however, and his efforts were not always successful. He intimidated the media, even the venerable *New York Times*. And he drew the public wrath of Eleanor Roosevelt when she was the nation's first lady; she viewed his campaign to obtain public funds for Catholic schools a breach of the American principle of church-state separation. To the often brow-beaten priests serving under him, Spellman was simply "The Boss," and the New York Archdiocese headquarters was "The Powerhouse." Unlike Cushing, he did not support John F. Kennedy's presidential bid in 1960, fearing that the young, charismatic Massachusetts senator could usurp his own coveted role as America's most prominent Catholic. Besides, the Kennedys' chief spiritual adviser was Cushing, not Spellman.

Spellman indeed lost a bit of his political clout during the brief time Kennedy was president. Yet he retained influence in the Vatican, and this helped him improve Catholic-Jewish relations. With his traditional religious beliefs and take-no-prisoners style of leadership, Spellman appeared an unlikely candidate to build better relations with Jews and to develop a new and more positive Catholic understanding of Judaism. Yet, it was Spellman, a child of small-town Protestant New England, who in his youth had limited contact with Jews and Judaism, and a man who spent many years living within the Vatican bubble, who provided needed momentum and support at a critical moment during the Second Vatican Council. Because of who Spellman was and the elements within the Church he represented, the cardinal's efforts were indispensable during the final efforts of the Vatican Council to adopt the *Nostra Aetate* declaration on the Jewish people.

Spellman and Silver: A "Beautiful Friendship"

One reason for Spellman's public support for *Nostra Aetate* can be traced to his long personal relationship with Charles H. Silver of New York. A longtime leader within New York's large Jewish community, Silver developed a mutually beneficial friendship with Spellman; the former gave the latter interreligious credibility in a pluralistic America, while the latter in return always had the ear of an extremely influential cardinal on issues important to Jews. Silver's was the classic story of Jewish immigrants to New York: born in Romania, he moved with his family at age 6 to the Lower East Side of Manhattan. As a youth he assisted his father in making men's suspenders; this led to a job as an office boy in a textile company. Eventually he was successful in the clothing industry, becoming vice president of the American Woolen Company. Eager to become something more than a wealthy clothing manufacturer, Silver served for thirty-five years as chairman of the annual Alfred E. Smith Memorial Dinner, a gala event that raises money for Catholic charities. In his turn, the cardinal of the city with the world's largest Jewish population recognized that he could not be the perceived adversary of either Jews or Protestants if he wanted to be successful in his many endeavors.

In return for Silver's efforts, Spellman, working as usual behind the scenes, made certain his Jewish friend was appointed to the New York City Board of Education in 1951 as the representative from the borough of Manhattan. Four years later, Silver, again thanks to Spellman, became president of the Board of Education, a position he held until 1961. The maneuver provided a friendly link between the "Boss" and the vast New York City public educational system.

Silver was a New York State delegate to several Democratic National Conventions, and in 1951 President Harry Truman appointed him to the Presidential Commission on Internal Security and Individual Rights that was chaired by World War II hero U.S.

Navy Admiral Chester W. Nimitz. The Commission was formed to rebut Senator Joseph McCarthy's notorious anti-Communist campaign of the period. Silver gave the pro-McCarthy New York Cardinal a set of friendly eyes and ears within the Commission itself. Silver was also a major supporter and longtime president of New York City's Beth Israel Hospital, and was also active in supporting Yeshiva University, its Einstein School of Medicine, and B'nai Jeshurun, a large Conservative synagogue in Manhattan.

While he was one of America's most prominent philanthropists, a member of a presidential commission, the president of the New York City Board of Education, and a financial supporter of many worthwhile charities, to many of Spellman's priests and Catholic lay leaders, Charlie Silver was simply "Spelly's Jew." Nevertheless, in that role Silver secured Spellman's assistance in Israel's 1949 campaign to gain membership in the United Nations. Less than a year after declaring independence on May 14, 1948, the Jewish state, after a bloody but successful War of Independence, applied for membership in the U.N. But in the spring of 1949, the Jewish state's request was opposed by a hostile coalition of Arab and Islamic countries as well as India. Complicating matters, a bloc of nearly twenty Latin and South American nations and the Philippines, all with large Catholic populations, were in the undecided column. Israel's status as a legitimate member of the international community hung in the balance.

In April 1949, a concerned Silver asked the cardinal to join him on a walk together on Manhattan's Fifth Avenue. The two often took such a stroll when they wished to discuss items of importance without being overheard by others. On this particular walk, Silver asked his friend to issue a public statement expressing support for Israel's bid for U.N. membership. Years later, Silver confessed he was not certain of the cardinal's view on the matter. This was because in 1949 the Vatican supported the internationalization of the city of Jerusalem (a position it has since abandoned) and because there were many in the highest levels of the

U.S. government and the Holy See who were cool, even hostile, to the creation of a Jewish state in the Middle East. Included in that group were Secretary of State George C. Marshall and Defense Secretary James Forrestal, both of whom worked with Spellman on diplomatic and national security issues. There were also rumors circulating at the time within the Catholic community that Jews desecrated Christian holy places in Israel and physically persecuted Christians. While such rumors were not true, they made Spellman's task of assisting Israel more difficult. As a result, Silver was unsure of how his friend might respond to his request regarding Israel's U.N. membership.

But Spellman's reply was positive: "I will do something that may mean a great deal more." He promised to call the U.N. delegates from Latin and South American countries as well as the Philippines and "share with them my fond wish" that Israel gain membership to the world body. Silver was elated: "[M]y heart seemed to stop beating. It was a terrific gesture." And in his typical style of operation, Spellman privately contacted the various delegations as he had promised.

The roll call vote to admit Israel to the U.N. took place a month later on May 11, 1949. The vote was 37-12 in favor with nine abstentions (including Great Britain, the Mandate power in pre-Israel Palestine for nearly thirty years following World War I). Of the 37 affirmative votes, including the U.S. and the Soviet Union, over half came from Argentina, Bolivia, Chile, Colombia, Costa Rico, Cuba, Dominican Republic, Ecuador, Guatemala, Haiti, Honduras, Mexico, Nicaragua, Panama, Paraguay, Peru, the Philippines, Uruguay, and Venezuela. El Salvador and Brazil, the nation with the world's largest Catholic population, both abstained.

Years later, at a 1964 public dinner in New York City with the cardinal in attendance, Silver revealed Spellman's successful efforts. Spellman neither acknowledged nor denied his vital role in obtaining U.N. membership for Israel. His spokesman said "modesty" prevented Spellman from discussing his work. But Spellman extracted a price for his efforts in behalf of Israel. That same year, 1949, the ambitious Silver wanted to run for mayor of New York. But he was dissuaded by Spellman, who desired a Catholic and not a Jew or a Protestant in City Hall to clean up the corruption of the administration of Mayor William O'Dwyer, a Catholic. Silver agreed to drop out of the race, and Vincent Impellitteri was elected mayor. Perhaps as a consolation prize, two years later Spellman helped his Jewish friend become president of the Board of Education.

Taken together — Israel and the U.N., the New York City mayoral race, and the Board of Education post — it was *Romanita* practiced to perfection by Spellman. The next time Spellman was asked to use his influence in behalf of Jews came during the Second Vatican Council. Unlike his unseen role in 1949 involving Israel, in 1964 Spellman stepped out from behind his usual self-imposed curtain of discretion and moved directly into the public arena. His support that year of a strong council declaration on Catholic-Jewish relations surprised some people, but it could not have surprised Charlie Silver, who had learned that Spellman was capable of producing "terrific gestures" with respect to Jews and Judaism. As it turned out, such a gesture was needed in the struggle to adopt *Nostra Aetate*.

In 1964 and 1965, during the twilight of his life and career, Francis Spellman did not offer Charlie Silver a free luxury car, nor did he use his photographic skills to create a gift portrait of his Jewish friend. Instead, Spellman performed one final important act as a star on the world stage he loved so much: he publicly committed himself and his Church to a new constructive relationship with Jews and Judaism.

CHAPTER SIX

The Second Vatican Council: Battleground and Breakthrough

———◦◎◦———

The Council's Beginnings

Many historians have called the Second Vatican Council the most important religious event of the twentieth century. Essentially, the council was a gathering of the world's Catholic bishops, who met each autumn in Rome from 1962 from 1965. Many such councils have taken place over the centuries; this one was called a "Vatican Council" because its sessions were held in St. Peter's Basilica in the Vatican.

For many Catholics today, particularly progressive Catholics, the term "Vatican Council" serves as a handy catch-all to describe the sixteen long-needed reforms and new teachings — especially those relating to Jews and Judaism, ecumenism, religious liberty, education, and liturgy — that emerged from the council. For more theologically conservative Catholics, however, the Vatican Council is seen as a negative development. They view it as an unnecessary, unwarranted, and dangerous capitulation to the outside forces of modernity, religious pluralism, and spiritual relativism, and as an abandonment of several long-held positions, including the belief that there is no salvation outside the Church.

Because of the strong feelings surrounding the Second Vatican

Council, it is easy to forget that it was preceded by a *First* Vatican Council, a gathering that took place nearly a century earlier. Convened by Pope Pius IX in December 1869, it lasted just under a year; its major outcome was the adoption of the dogma of papal infallibility. This doctrine, frequently misunderstood even by Catholics, does not suggest that a pope is always correct or never makes mistakes. Rather, it asserts that a pope is free from error when, acting in his role as the supreme pontiff of the Roman Catholic Church, he promulgates a teaching related to faith, divine revelation, or morals.

The Second Vatican Council was convened by Angelo Giuseppe Roncalli, who on October 20, 1958, was elected to succeed the recently deceased Pius XII. Roncalli chose John XXIII as his papal name. At the time of his election, it was widely assumed that the 77-year-old pope would be a caretaker, a preserver of the status quo, a largely inactive figure who would allow the Curia — the Vatican hierarchy and civil service — to preserve things as they were during the time of his predecessor.

Such predictions turned out to be wildly inaccurate. On January 25, 1959, a little more than three months after his election, John called for a Vatican Council that would chart the Church's future. At first the call received little attention, but the new pope's seriousness about it became apparent when he used a now-famous image to describe what he intended the council to accomplish: it must, he said, "throw open the windows of the Church and let the fresh air of the Spirit blow through." John was aware that these "windows" would not always remain open, and he wanted to seize the unique opportunity for major reforms presented by the twentieth century: its scientific and intellectual revolutions, its two World Wars, its experiments in totalitarianism, and the horror of the Holocaust. While Pius XII had instituted some changes in his nearly two decades as pope, by the early 1960s the Catholic Church was perceived by both friendly observers and severe critics as hidebound and in danger of becoming increasingly irrelevant in the modern era.

As representatives of an institution nearly 2,000 years old, the Catholic bishops who attended the council confronted an extraordinary number of critical issues during its sessions, seeking to inaugurate Church-wide reform while preserving a venerable tradition. They addressed questions of religious liberty and freedom of conscience, defined the parameters of ecumenism, improved Catholic education, reformed the sacred liturgy, engaged the contemporary secular world, developed a Church constitution, and changed the relationship between the pope and the world's cardinals.

Modernity was particularly challenging for Pius XII. In August 1950 he promulgated the encyclical *Humani generis,* which warned about "some false opinions threatening to undermine the foundations of Catholic Doctrine." The "false opinions" in question were those of some modern theologians, especially the Frenchmen Yves Congar, Jean Daniélou, and Henri de Lubac, and the German Karl Rahner. Rahner in particular is revered today as one of the most important theologians of the twentieth century, but all four were "disciplined" by the Vatican during Pius XII's pontificate. Similarly, four years after *Humani generis,* the Vatican compelled the American priest John Courtney Murray to stop teaching and writing publicly in support of religious liberty and freedom of conscience. (Murray obeyed, but continued to write privately on these themes.) Yet in a dramatic move that sent a clear signal throughout the Church and must have stunned many members of the Curia, John XXIII invited these five "dissidents" to serve as official advisors at the Vatican Council. In this role they were instrumental in the passage of various documents.

The Most Difficult Issue

Perhaps the most difficult task for the bishops at the Second Vatican Council was that of establishing a new, positive relationship between Catholicism and Judaism. The issue was especially high on John XXIII's agenda because of the Holocaust — the mass murder of six million Jews in the heart of Europe between 1933 and 1945. In his demand for change, the pope was joined by Cardinal Augustin Bea (1881-1968), a biblical scholar and the president of the Vatican Secretariat for Promoting Christian Unity. The two men believed it was imperative for the Church to discard its traditional adversarial stance and often negative beliefs about Jews and Judaism, and replace them with a constructive relationship built on mutual respect and knowledge.

Pius XII's record during the Holocaust years, including both his actions and inactions regarding the endangered Jews of Europe, remains a controversial and divisive issue. More than fifty years after his death, Pius's defenders and critics are engaged in a continuing dispute about the role of the wartime pope. Complicating matters is the fact that the Vatican has classified thousands of pages of archival documents pertaining to World War II. In February 2006 Benedict XVI opened the files of Pius XI, who was pope between 1922 and 1939. Within these are documents relating to the career of Eugenio Pacelli when he served as the papal nuncio in Germany between 1917 and 1929, and when he was the Vatican secretary of state prior to his election as pope in 1939. Yet until and unless all the relevant documents from the papacy of Pius XII are made available for study, it will be impossible to accurately assess his role in the Holocaust period.

In contrast, John XXIII's thoughts and actions in support of the Jews during this period are much more apparent. In the early years of World War II, Cardinal Roncalli served as the Vatican's apostolic delegate to Turkey and Greece, and in 1942 Pius XII transferred him to Paris as the nuncio, or ambassador, to France. During this time the future pope wrote these words about the Jewish victims of the Holocaust: "We are dealing with one of the great mysteries in the history of humanity. Poor children of Israel. Daily I hear their groans around me. They are relatives and fellow countrymen of Jesus." Using his Vatican credentials and diplomatic position, Roncalli saved thousands of Jews in various parts of Europe. In Hungary he collaborated with the Sisters of Zion, an order of Catholic women, to issue false baptism papers for Jewish children, so that they could "pass" as Catholics and escape deportation to Hitler's death camps. He also worked with Bulgaria's King Boris, an Eastern Orthodox Christian and lukewarm Nazi ally, to save most of that nation's Jewish community.

And when he became pope it became apparent that John XXIII was serious about officially changing the Catholic Church's relations with the Jewish people. In 1959, less than a year after his election, he personally removed the Latin phrase *pro fididis Judaeis,* "for the faithless Jews," from the traditional Good Friday prayer that seeks the conversion of Jews to Christianity. He was serious about the change: in 1963, during a Vatican Good Friday service, he interrupted a cardinal who out of habit had recited the old version of the prayer. The pope stopped the service and demanded, "Say it over the new way." Similarly, in 1960 he greeted a group of Jews visiting the Vatican with a phrase from the book of Genesis: "I am Joseph, your brother." This was a reference to the pope's given name, Giuseppe. More deeply, though, it was an appropriation of the words of reconciliation the biblical patriarch Joseph had spoken to his separated brothers.

Reflecting the Church's growing size, especially in the Americas, Africa, and Asia, a total of 2,908 bishops were invited to the opening of the Second Vatican Council. It is interesting to note that among these were four future popes: Giovanni Battista Montini (1897-1978), who succeeded John XXIII as Paul VI in 1963; Albino Luciani (1912-1978), who died only thirty-three days after becoming John Paul I; Karol Wojtyla (1920-2005), who achieved larger-than-life status as John Paul II; and a 35-year-old German priest, Joseph Ratzinger, who in 2005 became Benedict XVI.

Latin Usage During the Council

Of course, the schedule of annual plenary sessions made "frequent fliers" of many bishops, but more than the lengthy travel time to Rome, what made the bishops' work particularly difficult was the use of Latin as the official language during council sessions. Why Latin? There remains a lingering suspicion among some Catholics that because the Curia opposed John XXIII's progressive initiatives, they imposed Latin in order to confuse the many bishops who could not follow deliberations in the ancient language. Making Latin the council's official language thus lessened the possibility of enacting reforms and real change within the Church. The official reason given, however, was that Latin, the Church's liturgical language, was a unifying element, even though centuries earlier it had ceased to be a daily vernacular anywhere in the world.

Cardinal Richard Cushing was among those who had difficulty understanding deliberations in Latin. Ever the pragmatist, he offered to underwrite the expense required to provide simultaneous translations of council deliberations into various languages, akin to the practice of the United Nations, but his proposal was never accepted. One reason for this was a fear that the use of languages other than Latin might result in council sessions being too easily understood outside the walls of St. Peter's. On the other hand, some exceptions were made: certain bishops from nations outside Europe were permitted to address the council in French.

The Second Vatican Council was not only a linguistic challenge; it was also an exhausting spiritual and emotional experience for its participants, who recognized that their actions and decisions constituted major changes for the Catholic Church. Much of the council's substantive work took place "off the floor," in the months between the autumn plenary gatherings. This work involved Vatican officials and their staffs, as well as special theological advisors known as *periti*.

One of those advisors was 32-year-old Father William H. Keeler of Harrisburg, Pennsylvania, who years later became a cardinal and served as archbishop of Baltimore between 1989 and 2007. During his career, Keeler was an internationally recognized leader in Catholic-Jewish relations, and served for many years as the chair of the United States Conference of Catholic Bishops Commission for Ecumenical and Interreligious Affairs. In 1992, he was elected by his fellow bishops to serve as the Conference's president. Keeler, an expert on canon law, attended all four sessions of the Second Vatican Council as an advisor to Bishop George Leech of Harrisburg. His memories of those sessions convey a sense of the great figures present. He recalls Bishop Karol Wojtyla of Poland, the future John Paul II, as speaking "with great clarity." He also once encountered Francis Spellman at an airport, and the young priest from Pennsylvania was impressed by one of the cardinal's best-known traits: "He had a great facility for remembering names and he called me 'Father Keeler.'" Keeler was also present as Pope John XXIII faced imminent death: "He spoke to the bishops and others inside Clementine Hall [a sixteenth-century chamber that is part of the Apostolic Palace] at the Vatican. The pope said: 'My bags are packed.' He was ready to go." The pope died of stomach cancer on June 3, 1963.

Jews and Judaism: First Steps

On September 20, 1960, two years before the formal opening of the Second Vatican Council, John XXIII directed Cardinal Bea to prepare a positive statement on Jews and Judaism for presentation and adoption by the bishops. Keeler recalls that Bea, during the council's first session, predicted any declaration on that subject would be a "footnote" and not a "freestanding document"; however, the Declaration on Jews and Judaism that was ultimately approved by the world's bishops five years later is today considered a major achievement, and hardly a footnote.

Despite John XXIII's optimistic predictions, it was not smooth sailing. Some bishops were opposed to any statement on Jews, and Cardinal Bea's first draft on Catholic-Jewish relations would have to undergo numerous revisions in order to gain council approval. In the end, the vetted and carefully crafted words of *Nostra Aetate* that were finally adopted on October 28, 1965, went through a series of complex and controversial drafts.

It was an enormous task for the Roman Catholic Church to make systemic changes in its encounter with the Jewish people and Judaism. Yet the leadership of John XXIII and of his successor, Paul VI, inspired a host of Catholic clergy and laity in many parts of the world to join together to achieve purposeful change throughout all sectors of the Church. In that pioneering effort they were joined by like-minded rabbis and lay Jewish men and women who were equally committed to building mutual respect and knowledge between the two ancient faith communities.

The Second Vatican Council differed from earlier councils in part because it attracted global attention from the print and electronic media, and also because representatives from Jewish, Protestant, and Eastern Orthodox communities attended many of its sessions as official guests or designated observers. Among these guests was Abraham Joshua Heschel (1907-1972), one of the twentieth century's most prominent rabbis, who discussed the future of Catholic-Jewish relations in a series of personal meetings with Paul VI and Cardinal Bea.

Heschel and Bea struck up an instant friendship based on their shared knowledge and love of the Bible, their European roots, and their shared belief that the Vatican Council offered a never-to-be-repeated opportunity to achieve a sea change in Catholic-Jewish relations. In January 1962 Bea asked Heschel for a detailed memorandum on ways to strengthen relations between Catholics and Jews. Heschel conveyed the cardinal's request to the American Jewish Committee (AJC) and the Anti-Defamation League, and both organizations presented documents to Vatican officials. In March 1963 the AJC hosted another consultation with Bea in New York City, and in September 1964, two days before Judaism's most sacred holy day of Yom Kippur, Heschel met with Paul VI in Rome. The rabbi urged the pope to officially repudiate the charge of deicide, and to delete references to conversion in any proposed document. Heschel is reported to have told the pope, "If faced with the choice of baptism or the crematoria of Auschwitz, I would choose Auschwitz."

By 1964 both the pope and the rabbi were aware of the anti-Jewish elements that were active within the Church and the council itself. Primary among these was a coalition of mainly European bishops who clung to traditional beliefs hostile to Jews and Judaism, particularly the notion that Christianity had fulfilled the spiritual vocation of Judaism, so that the latter no longer played a viable role in the divine economy. This group was joined in Rome by prelates from the Middle East who believed that any statement on Jews, no matter how tepid, would be perceived in their region as tantamount to Catholic political support for the Jewish state of Israel that had achieved independence in 1948. Opponents of a council statement on Jews, whether grounded in theological anti-Judaism or political anti-Zionism, "made a lot of noise," Keeler recalls. Nevertheless, they were few in number and they ultimately failed to prevent passage of the Declaration on the Jews.

Bea's various drafts of the document reveal not only his own thinking, but also that of John XXIII and Paul VI. They also make clear the kinds of subtle changes that were required to ensure its eventual passage. Bea's first draft was completed in November 1961, before the council began. It combines positive teachings about the Jewish people with traditional Catholic language about the Church's "unshaken faith and deep longing" that Jews will eventually convert and become members of the Church. Bea wrote:

> The Church, the Bride of Christ, acknowledges with a heart
> full of gratitude that, according to God's mysterious saving

design, the beginnings of her faith and election go as far back as to the Israel of the Patriarchs and Prophets. . . . The Church, in fact, believes that Christ, who "is our peace," embraces Jews and Gentiles with one and the same love and that He made the two one (see Eph. 2:14). She rejoices that the union of these two "in one body" (Eph. 2:16) proclaims the whole world's reconciliation in Christ. Even though the greater part of the Jewish people has remained separated from Christ, it would be an injustice to call this people accursed, since they are greatly beloved for the sake of the Fathers and the promises made to them (see Rom. 11:28). The Church loves this people. From them sprang Christ the Lord, who reigns in glory in heaven; from them sprang the Virgin Mary, mother of all Christians; from them came the Apostles, the pillars and bulwark of the Church (1 Tim. 3:15). . . . Furthermore, the Church believes in the union of the Jewish people with herself as an integral part of Christian hope. With unshaken faith and deep longing the Church awaits union with this people. . . . [The Church] condemns most severely injustices committed against innocent people everywhere, so she raises her voice in loud protest against all wrongs done to Jews, whether in the past or in our time. Whoever despises or persecutes this people does injury to the Catholic Church.

Bea sensed that this "balanced" first draft, with its attempts to accommodate both sides, would in fact please no one, and so he made certain it was never brought to a vote on the council floor. A revised, second draft was given to the council on November 8, 1963, five months after John XXIII's death, but it too was never voted on. This second draft departed from its predecessor in that it contained a specific condemnation of the charge of deicide against the Jewish people, which Heschel and others wanted the council to specifically repudiate. It also softened references to

Catholic hopes for the eventual conversion of the Jews to Christianity. It urged priests to refrain from doing or saying anything that created "hatred or contempt" toward Jews, and it promoted "theological studies and fraternal discussions" between Catholics and Jews.

The inclusion of the word "contempt" reflects the influence of Jules Isaac (1877-1963), a French historian and Legion of Honor winner, who served as the inspector-general of that nation's public educational system during the 1930s. He successfully hid from the Germans when France was occupied during World War II, although his wife and daughter were deported and killed at Auschwitz. In the postwar years, Isaac concentrated on the religious roots of religious anti-Semitism; he was the first to use the phrase "teaching of contempt," a phrase which has now entered into the lexicon of interreligious dialogue, to describe negative Christian teaching and preaching about Jews and Judaism. Isaac stressed three major anti-Jewish teachings that have been employed throughout history: first, that the physical dispersion of Jews was God's punishment because they did not accept Jesus as the Messiah; second, that as "Christ killers," Jews committed the crime of deicide; third, that the static Judaism of the first Christian century was spiritually empty of any authentic meaning.

Isaac had a meeting with Pius XII in 1949, and eleven years later he met with John XXIII; both meetings took place at the Vatican. On each occasion Isaac presented his findings and urged the elimination of all "teaching of contempt" from the Catholic Church. While his encounter with Pius XII did not bring about real change, he fared better with John XXIII, who entered into a fulsome conversation with the 83-year-old Holocaust survivor. Isaac's scholarly research and personal commitment impressed the pope, who understood and internalized his teachings. Thus many of his views appear in the various drafts and in the final version of the Declaration on the Jews, even though Isaac, who died in 1963, did not live to see its adoption.

Bea's Balancing Act

But after writing two drafts that were never voted on, Bea began to recognize the futility of balancing positive statements and teachings about Jews and Judaism with traditional hopes for conversion. The bishops at the council who opposed any outreach to Jews rebuffed Bea's positive language, while more progressive ones rejected any calls for conversion. Jewish leaders, not surprisingly, stood in solidarity with the latter group, believing that Judaism was indeed an authentic, "perfected" religion and remembering all too well the centuries when hostile conversion efforts were more than rhetorical.

Bea's second draft includes these paragraphs, urging

> cooperation with people who are not Christians, who, nevertheless, worship God, or at least in a spirit of good will conscientiously endeavor to observe the moral law innate in human nature. . . . This applies especially in the case of the Jews, who as a people are connected with the Church of Christ in a special relationship. The Church of Christ acknowledges with a grateful heart that the beginnings of the faith and of its election, along with the saving mystery of God, can already be found among the Patriarchs and Prophets. For all the believers in Christ, the sons of Abraham according to the faith (cf. Gal. 3:7), are included in the vocation of that same Patriarch. . . . The Church, a new creature in Christ (cf. Eph. 2:15), cannot forget that it is a continuation of that people with whom of old God, out of his ineffable mercy, was pleased to make his Old Covenant. . . . In addition the Church believes that Christ, our Peace, embraced both Jews and Gentiles in a single love and made them one (cf. Eph. 2:14) and by the union of both in one body (cf. Eph. 2:17) announced the reconciliation of the entire world in Christ. Although a large part of the Chosen People

is still far from Christ, yet it is wrong to call them an accursed people, since they remain very dear to God because of the Fathers and the gifts given them (cf. Rom. 11:28), or a deicidal people, since the Lord, by his passion and death, washes away the sins of all men, which were the cause of the passion and death of Jesus Christ (cf. Luke 23:34; Acts 3:17; 1 Cor. 2:8). The death of Christ is not to be attributed to an entire people then alive, and even less to a people today. Therefore, let priests be careful not to say anything, in catechetical instruction or in preaching, that might give rise to hatred or contempt of the Jews in the hearts of their hearers. Nor does the Church forget that Christ Jesus was born of that people according to the flesh, that the Virgin Mary, the Mother of Christ, was thus born, that thus were born the Apostles, the foundation and pillars of the Church.

Therefore, since the Church has so much of a common patrimony with the Synagogue, this Holy Synod intends in every way to promote and further mutual knowledge and esteem obtained by theological studies and fraternal discussions; and, moreover, as it severely reproves injuries to people anywhere, even more so does it, with maternal heart, deplore and condemn hatred and persecution of Jews, whether committed of old or in our own times.

This draft makes direct reference to the charge of deicide — a reference Bea deleted in response to continuing pressure from certain bishops. One of these, Cardinal Ernesto Ruffini of Sicily, argued that because "deicide" was not an official teaching of the Church, council participants by definition could not vote on the concept. Ruffini and others further argued that "deicide" was theologically impossible since God can never be killed. Yet there were others who, conscious of how the charge of "Christ-killers" had been used over the centuries, were alarmed by the deletion. Yet while this draft refers directly to deicide, it does not contain the term "anti-Semitism" for hatred of Jews and Judaism. Many people hoped that the council would specifically repudiate the pathology of anti-Semitism by name in the Declaration. The term was coined in 1879 by the reactionary German writer and journalist Wilhelm Marr (1819-1904), who wanted a "scientific" basis for his hatred of Jews and Judaism, rather than a "religious" one. "Anti-Semitism" was meant to serve as a respectable, "academic" substitute for the more direct term "anti-Jewish." Prior to this there had never been a "Semitism" for Marr to attach his "anti-" to, but that did not stop the term from becoming a toxic euphemism for bigotry and prejudice, as well as a potent Nazi battle cry.

Bea released his third draft in 1964. Titled "On Jews and Non-Christians," it was much longer than its two predecessors. Two years into the council, there was a new pope, Paul VI, and the battle lines among the bishops regarding the proposed statement on Jews and Judaism had become clear. Everyone at the council knew this was an issue that would define the Church for generations to come, and many prelates were under increasing pressure to scuttle the proposed Declaration. But they also understood that the whole world was watching their actions. The stakes could not have been higher. In a strategic move that ultimately proved successful, Bea folded the draft text about Jews into a larger "Schema on Ecumenism" that included references to Muslims and members of other faith communities.

During the spring and summer of 1964 Bea, his staff, and the bishops struggled with the revised wording of the proposed Declaration. This third draft repudiated all forms of prejudice against Jews, though it did so without using the term "anti-Semitism." It also implicitly rejected the deicide charge. And it urged Catholics to foster mutual respect and understanding with Jews after nearly two millennia of misunderstanding, suspicion, distrust, and a lack of accurate knowledge about one another. It includes this wording:

The Church of Christ gladly acknowledges that the beginnings of its faith and election, in accordance with God's mystery of salvation, are to be found already among the Patriarchs and Prophets. Indeed, all Christians believe that, as sons of Abraham by faith (cf. Gal. 3:7), they are included in this Patriarch's vocation. . . . Nor can the Church as a new creation in Christ (cf. Eph. 2:15) and as the people of the New Covenant forget that it is a continuation of that people with whom God in his ineffable mercy once designed to enter into the Old Covenant and to whom he chose to entrust the revelation contained in the Books of the Old Testament.

Moreover, the Church does not forget that from this Jewish people were born Christ, the Virgin Mary, as well as the apostles, the foundation and the pillars of the Church.

Further, the Church was always mindful and will never overlook Apostle Paul's words relating to the Jews, to whom belong "the adoption as sons and the glory, and the covenants and the giving of the law, and the worship, and the promises" (Rom. 9:4).

Since such is the inheritance accepted by Christians from the Jews, this Holy Council is resolved expressly to further and to recommend mutual understanding and appreciation, to be obtained by theological study and fraternal discussion and, beyond that, just as it severely disapproves of any wrong inflicted upon human beings everywhere, it also deplores and condemns hatred and maltreatment of Jews.

It is also worth remembering that the union of the Jewish people with the Church is a part of the Christian hope. Accordingly, and following the teaching of Apostle Paul (cf. Rom. 11:25), the Church expects in unshakable faith and with ardent desire the entrance of that people into the fullness of the people of God established by Christ.

Everyone should be careful, therefore, not to present the Jewish people as a rejected nation, whether in catechetical instruction, in preaching of God's Word or in daily conversation. Neither should anything be said or done that could alienate human minds from the Jews. Equally, all should be on their guard not to impute to the Jews of our time that which was perpetrated in the Passion of Christ. . . . But we surely cannot appeal or pray to God as the Father of all, if we deny brotherly behavior to some people who are all created in the image of God. . . .

Impelled by such love for our brothers, let us consider with great diligence views and doctrines which, though in many points are different from ours, in so many others, however, carry the ray of that truth which gives light to every person born into this world. Thus we embrace also, and first of all, the Moslems who worship one personal and recompensing God and who in religious feeling as well as through many channels of human culture come near to us.

In consequence, any theory or practice which leads to discrimination among individuals or between nation and nation, insofar as human dignity and the rights flowing therefrom are concerned, is devoid of foundation.

It is imperative, therefore, that all people of good will and Christians in particular abstain from any discrimination or abuse of human beings on grounds of their race, color, social status or religion. On the contrary, this Holy Council solemnly entreats believing Christians "to maintain friendly relations among the gentiles" (1 Pet. 2:12) and if possible and insofar as it depends on them, to maintain peace with all people (cf. Rom. 12:18).

This draft reached the council floor and was the subject of a full debate on September 28-29, 1964. It still contained language that spoke of Jews ultimately converting and entering the Catholic Church. It deleted the word "deicidal," and the term "anti-Semitism" does not appear. The retention of conversion language was perceived by many observers as a final attempt to satisfy the small bloc of anti-Jewish bishops. Yet if Bea believed the inclusion of such traditional language would quell his opposition, he was wrong. There was still a strong attack on the proposed document.

The American Cardinals

The council deliberations in late September 1964 cannot be understood without taking into account some of the major events leading up to those two days of intense debate — events which involved Cardinals Richard Cushing of Boston and Francis Spellman of New York.

In the early months of 1964, Cushing, Spellman, and other likeminded American bishops, including Cardinal Albert Meyer of Chicago, Cardinal Joseph Ritter of St. Louis, and Bishop Stephen Leven of San Antonio, became alarmed by reports that the statement on Jews and Judaism might be doomed — either defeated outright in a vote, or more likely tabled and permanently buried. They sensed that Cardinal Bea was discouraged by the continuing opposition to his proposals and by the death of John XXIII. While Paul VI supported his predecessor's commitment to improving relations with Jews, he lacked John XXIII's personal charisma and the affection and esteem of millions of people around the globe.

Cushing and Spellman, the most prominent Catholic leaders in the United States, acted each in their own way to prevent such potential disasters. The two men represented two different segments of the Catholic Church in America. The New York archbishop, the "Boss," was more feared than loved. With silky smooth efficiency, he moved at the highest levels of the Church and the American government, and because of his travels as a Catholic chaplain to the U.S. armed forces, he commanded media attention throughout the world. In contrast, many of Cushing's travels away from Boston took him to South America, where he was active in working with children who had learning and physical disabilities. Yet in spite of their differences, both men were acting at a moment in history when the Church and Catholicism could finally have been said to have "arrived" in the U.S. Their actions in favor of Jews and Judaism came less than a year after the assassination of John F. Kennedy, America's first Catholic president, and the nation's great outpouring of love and emotion for the slain leader.

Cushing, of course, was intimately connected to the Kennedy family. After the president's death he immediately became a beloved, highly visible Church leader, even finding himself the subject of a *Time* magazine cover story. And it was widely perceived that he "represented" the views of the martyred president and his famous family. That perception afforded Cushing enormous credibility and influence.

Spellman's impact upon the Vatican Council and its deliberations was more subtle, but no less powerful than Cushing's. During the "Spellman years," the New York archdiocese was the largest in the United States in membership (it has since been supplanted by the Los Angeles archdiocese). Spellman, a master wielder of both spiritual and temporal power, had cultivated personal friendships with a number of prominent American Jewish leaders in New York City, contacts that were of benefit to both Spellman and to the Jewish community. And until J.F.K.'s election to the presidency in 1960, the archbishop of New York was the most recognized and influential Catholic in America, a position he coveted and cultivated.

There was another factor that provided both Cushing and Spellman with added prestige and influence when they pressed for a revolution in Catholic-Jewish relations: the growing public awareness in the 1960s of the Holocaust and the undeniable fact that millions of baptized Christians, including many Roman Catholics, had willingly participated in mass murder and genocide in the heart of what a later pope, John Paul II, called "Christian Europe." Many of the bishops at the Vatican Council, including John XXIII, had personally experienced World War I, and all of them had lived through World War II. The loss of life, property, and self-confidence in both wars was staggering. The bishops in the 1960s were well acquainted with toxic nationalism, atomic bombs, genocide, and totalitarianism.

In addition, Europe, the home continent of many prelates, was still physically and spiritually exhausted both from war and from the work of rebuilding itself. Meanwhile, the United States had emerged as a superpower whose mainland had remained untouched during both global conflicts, and America's large Christian communities were untainted by any direct complicity in the Holocaust.

Thus when Cushing and Spellman demanded changes in the Church's teaching, preaching, and perception of Jews and Judaism, they did so with powerful voices that commanded attention. The two cardinals represented a wealthy nation that had successfully led a "crusade" — General Dwight Eisenhower, the Supreme Allied Commander in Europe, used this medieval Christian term in his 1948 book *Crusade in Europe* — against Nazism and Fascism, and in 1964 it was the United States that led the opposition to the atheistic Communist doctrines of the Soviet Union. Simply put, when the leaders of America's Catholic Church spoke, the world's bishops, whatever their own views on Jews and Judaism, were compelled to listen. Like the war-weary European continent itself, Pope Paul VI, Cardinal Bea, and other Vatican leaders required the fresh energy and strength that came from the so-called "New World."

To succeed, Cushing and Spellman employed a dual strategy, both public and private, to guarantee the passage of the Declaration on Jews and Judaism. Spellman made the first move. In a dramatic departure, the New York archbishop delivered a major speech in New York City on April 30, 1964, at the American Jewish Committee's annual meeting. In it, the cardinal addressed the Church's urgent need to change its relationship with Jews and Judaism. It was a radical departure for the always cautious Spellman, who generally preferred to work behind the scenes. Until the AJC speech, in a packed Hilton Hotel ballroom, Spellman had not spoken so directly on the subjects of anti-Semitism and deicide, at least not publicly. Spellman's clear, unambiguous remarks gained headlines around the world.

A Taxi Driver's Question

To no one's surprise, Spellman's language was neither theologically complex nor strewn with references to the Bible or the Church Fathers. The cardinal, of course, mentioned his close friend and confidant Pius XII, as well as Pius XI and John XXIII (whom Spellman personally disdained, in fact). His central image was the familiar example of a New York City taxi driver. Ultimately, it was not important how Spellman reached his conclusions; rather, it was the speaker himself and what he said that provided instant credibility for Catholics, indeed for all Christians, to oppose the twin evils of anti-Semitism and the deicide canard:

> one remembers how often and how unjustly the Jewish people have suffered from slander and oppression. . . . [W]e are all children of God and indeed our brothers' keepers. That we are our brothers' keepers is more than a pious cliché. It is a lesson the whole world sorely needs to learn. As a matter of fact it has become an imperative for survival in our day. By every means at our disposal we must wage war on the old suspicions and prejudices and bigotry which have set brother against brother and have spawned a brood of evils threatening the very existence of our society. Definitely we must win that war.
>
> The sad plight of minorities in many places bears testimony to the existence of racial and religious prejudice. The

struggle of millions of American Negroes to achieve first class citizenship underscores it. The shameful murder in this very generation of 6,000,000 Jews and of millions of other innocent victims of tyranny proclaims it. The widespread oppression of Catholic and Protestants and other religious groups both now and throughout the past tells a story of prejudice that darkens the pages of history. Prejudice is mysterious and its roots are deeply buried. No rational being can fully understand it or comprehend all the reasons behind it. But one thing I do know: prejudice can never be justified by the teachings of religion. Hatred can never be justified by those teachings.

The Founder of my Faith gave one supreme commandment to all who would follow Him: "By this shall all men know that you are my disciples, if you have love for one another." This point needs stressing in the light of a recent survey examining the reasons behind anti-Semitism. Asked why the Jewish people have often suffered outbreaks of persecution, a surprising number of people replied that in their opinion it was a punishment for their part in the Crucifixion of Christ. Frankly I was appalled. This is not Christianity. I don't know where they learned it, but surely it was not from the teaching of their church. It is one of those distorted and terribly harmful notions which somehow gain currency and like a cancer spread among certain people who wish to justify their own bigotry.

The question of responsibility for the Crucifixion of Christ must be carefully stated and clearly understood. I am reminded of an incident which happened to a priest of my acquaintance when he was riding in a taxicab here one day last year. The cab drivers of New York, as everyone knows, are celebrated for their conversational talents. Not infrequently they emerge as homespun philosophers and this particular driver was even a sort of sidewalk theologian. Over his shoulder he said to the priest: "I understand that those Bishops over in Rome are saying that everyone who ever lived is responsible for the death of Our Lord. Does that mean that the poor Indians who were hunting buffalo on the plains of America at the time were responsible? Why, they didn't even know it was happening, how could they be responsible?"

He asked a good question, to which there is only one answer. Responsibility for the Crucifixion of Jesus as an event of history belongs only to those individuals who were present at the time and who cooperated in His death. It is simply absurd to maintain that there is some kind of continuing guilt which is transferred to any group and which rests upon them as a curse for which they must suffer. The Christian faith, on the other hand, does teach that Christ Our Savior died for all of us, in expiation for the sins of all mankind. In this sense we do believe that we are all mystically implicated in His death, but all without exception and all in the same way. And his dying for us must never be thought of as a curse upon anyone, but rather as a blessing upon all. . . . Anti-Semitism can never find a basis in the Catholic religion. Far from emphasizing the differences which divide Jews from Christians, our Faith stresses our common origins and the ties which bind us together. In the early days of Nazism, when the wave of anti-Semitism threatened to engulf Europe, Pope Pius XI stated clearly: "Abraham is our Patriarch, our ancestor. Anti-Semitism is not compatible with this sublime reality. It is a movement in which we Christians cannot share. Spiritually we are Semites." I recall well quoting those words in my broadcast to the Hungarian leaders and their people in June of 1944, a broadcast which I made at the request of Pope Pius XII to protest the bloody persecution of Hungarian Jews. I reminded them that their action was "in direct contradiction to the Catholic Faith" and I told them that "no one who hates can be a follower of the gentle

Christ, and no man can love God and hate his brother. . . ." St.
Paul tells us that the Jews are our brothers. This is the teaching of the Catholic Church and it can never be otherwise. My
friends, God is love, and his will for all of us is fraternal charity and understanding. It is high time that all, Christians and
Jews alike, applied this great religious principle to their
dealings with one another. It is high time to stress the bonds
of brotherhood which should characterize our relationship.
The beloved Pope John XXIII taught the world a lesson
which I pray it will neither ignore nor forget, when in greet-
ing a delegation of Jewish visitors to the Vatican . . . he
opened wide his arms and said: "I am Joseph, your brother."
In that one simple gesture, springing from his great heart, he
proclaimed to the world the true meaning of the Christian
spirit. . . . Let us try to understand one another better — little by little, step by step, to accept our differences and to respect one another's convictions; to attack prejudice where
first we may encounter it, within our own mind and heart.
And having conquered it there, let us go forth. . . .

A speech like this by any other bishop in the world would not have
attracted the same attention. Of course, some of the reactions
were negative — that Spellman had somehow sold out the
Church, or was a "Jew lover," or worse. But precisely because Francis Spellman was perceived as the leader of American Catholics
and because he had impeccable credentials as a political and
theological conservative, it was impossible for most Catholics to
simply dismiss his views as those of an extreme progressive, or to
ignore them. Indeed, one Catholic who shared them was Paul VI:
a month after Spellman's address, the pope said to an American
Jewish Committee leadership delegation, "Cardinal Spellman had
spoken my sentiments and his views coincide with and are identi-
cal with mine." These remarks dealt a body blow to the anti-
Jewish forces at the Vatican Council.

Spellman's address turned out to be the first of a one-two punch that energized the faltering supporters of a strong Vatican Council statement and stunned its opponents. The second punch came from Richard Cushing. Unlike Spellman, Cushing had been an admirer of John XXIII, and with the pope's death in 1963 he began to worry that no statement would be adopted. He had a number of reasons to be supportive of positive Catholic-Jewish relations: his leading role in the excommunication of the anti-Semitic Father Leonard Feeney, his warm relationship with his Jewish brother-in-law, and his distinctly American Catholicism. And he sensed that even the strong and unexpected advocacy of Spellman, while certainly welcome, may not have been enough to ensure a successful outcome. He decided he had to travel to Rome and address the council directly. But what would he say and how would he say it?

The Speech of His Life

On June 19, 1964, Cushing wrote a letter to a fellow native of Massachusetts, Father Walter Abbott, a Jesuit scholar who lived in New York City. Abbott was a former editor of *America,* the Jesuit magazine. In his letter, Cushing asked Abbott to

> prepare for me in English a brief statement on "Liberty of Conscience" and our relationship with the Jews. . . . These statements will make or mar [the] Vatican Council. I happen to know the Holy Father thinks as I do on these questions, but he must have support. . . . The statements should be brief; that is . . . surely not more than eight minutes to read. When I have these statements and approve them, I can call upon one of the local [Boston] Jesuits to put them for me in Latin. . . . I do not wish to give this assignment to any of the secular priests of the Archdiocese of Boston, because,

like myself, they do not keep anything a secret. . . . I am one hundred per cent behind the statement that . . . directly or indirectly we do not condemn the Jews of our day or of the past of the crime of deicide. . . . Live or die . . . I have resolved to speak on both topics. This is the only favor of its kind that I ever asked of the Jesuits. . . . [I]n the name of the Church help me. . . .

It was, of course, a request Father Abbott could not and did not refuse. The Boston cardinal surely knew that his words, in whatever language, would be widely reported. As he neared his seventieth birthday, he was ready for his "prime time" moment in St. Peter's.

On September 18, 1964, the *New York Times* reported that Cushing presided at a meeting in Rome that included 170 of America's 240 bishops, who "decided unanimously to work for improvement of draft declarations on the Jews and religious liberty." Five days later Cushing addressed the council on the latter topic and his remarks "were greeted with a storm of applause." But he was not done. He had one more speech to give, and it would be the most important and widely reported one of his life. On September 28 Cushing addressed the world's bishops for the second time within a week. The two speeches — one on religious liberty and the other on the Declaration on the Jews — were the only public speeches he made during the four-year council.

Because Spellman was ill that autumn and did not attend the council, it was left to Cushing to lead the forces not only of the United States but of all bishops with similar views from other parts of the globe. In his council address, Cushing spoke about the evil of anti-Semitism and the need for the Church to rid itself of a terrible prejudice that insulted Jews and debilitated the Church. Like Spellman's New York City speech a few months earlier, Cushing's remarks, delivered in Latin with the cardinal's raspy, heavy New England accent, drew wide attention and exhilarated many council participants. One observer recalled that Cushing's strong voice shattered the microphones and echoed throughout the vast Basilica. There was huge applause when he finished.

He declared:

The Declaration on the Jews and non-Christians is acceptable in general. Through this Ecumenical Council the church must manifest to the whole world, and to all men, a concern which is genuine, an esteem all embracing, a sincere charity — in a word, it must show forth Christ. And in this Schema "De Ecumenismo," with its declarations on religious liberty and on the Jews and non-Christians, in a certain sense it does just that. I would propose, however, three amendments specifically on the Jews.

First: We must make our statement about Jews more positive, less timid, more charitable. Our text well illustrates the priceless patrimony which the new Israel has received from the law and the prophets.

And it well illustrates what the Jews and Christians share in common. But surely we ought to indicate the fact that we sons of Abraham according to the spirit must show a special esteem and particular love for the sons of Abraham according to the flesh because of this common patrimony. As sons of Adam, they are our brothers: as sons of Abraham, they are the blood brothers of Christ.

The fourth paragraph of the declaration should manifest this and our obligation of special esteem, as a conclusion which logically flows from the first section.

Secondly: On the culpability of the Jews for the death of our Saviour. As we read in sacred scriptures, the rejection of the Messiah by his own people is a mystery: a mystery which is indeed for our instruction, not for exaltation.

The parables and prophecies of our Lord teach us this. We cannot judge the leaders of ancient Israel — God alone is their judge. And most certainly we cannot dare attribute to later generations of Jews the guilt of the crucifixion of the Lord Jesus or the death of the Saviour of the world, except in the sense of the universal guilt in which all of us men share.

We know and we believe that Christ died freely, and he died for all men and because of the sins of all men, Jews and gentiles.

Therefore, in this declaration, in clear and evident words, we must deny that the Jews are guilty of the death of our Saviour except insofar as all men have sinned and on that account crucified him and, indeed, still crucify him. And especially, we must condemn any who would attempt to justify inequities, hatred or even persecution of the Jews as Christian actions.

All of us have seen the evil fruit of this kind of false reasoning. In this august assembly, in this solemn moment, we must cry out: There is no Christian rationale — neither theological nor historical — for any inequity, hatred or persecution of our Jewish brothers.

Great is the hope, both among Catholics and among our separated Christian brothers, as well as among our Jewish friends in the New World, that this sacred synod will make such a fitting declaration.

Thirdly and finally: I ask, venerable brothers, whether we ought not to confess humbly before the world that Christians too frequently have not shown themselves as true Christians, as faithful to Christ, in their relations with their Jewish brothers? In this our age, how many have suffered! How many have died because of the indifference of Christians, because of silence! There is no need to enumerate the crimes committed in our own time. If not many Christian voices were lifted in recent years against the great injustices, yet let our voices humbly cry out now.

Rabbi Marc H. Tanenbaum, the American Jewish Committee's interreligious affairs director at the time, later wrote:

> If nothing else came out of Vatican Council II other than what took place in Rome on September 28 and 29, 1964, the Council more than justified its existence. . . . [T]hirty-one cardinals and bishops from every continent took positions regarding Catholic attitudes in relation to the Jewish people, Judaism, the role of Israel in salvation history, the synagogue and its continued relevance, conversion, anti-Semitism — positions that have never been heard before. . . . [A] profound turning point had taken place.

Likewise, Cardinal Keeler believes the positive American experience with religious pluralism had much to do with the strong positions taken by Cushing, Spellman, and other Catholic leaders from the U.S. For them, Jews and Judaism were not a metaphysical construction. Keeler also believes American public opinion was important in ensuring the passage of *Nostra Aetate*.

Having made their strong public interventions, Cushing and Spellman also pressed their positions behind the scenes. Their public and private efforts influenced other Catholic leaders to speak up and support their efforts. And they provided the newly elected Paul VI with the backing he needed. John XXIII, Paul VI, Cardinal Bea, and others had moved the ball (a Church-wide positive Declaration on Catholic-Jewish relations) close to the desired goal line (the council's final positive vote on the statement). However, a final push was required, and Cushing and Spellman provided it. On October 28, 1965, the bishops at the Second Vatican Council adopted the now historic *Nostra Aetate* ("In Our Time") Declaration on Jews and Judaism. The final vote was overwhelming: 2,221 in favor and only 88 bishops in opposition. To complete the metaphor, Cushing and Spellman moved the ball into the end zone.

624 Words Make History

The English version of *Nostra Aetate* is only 624 words in length. A whiff of the original conversionary language still remains embedded in the text; while the word "deicide" was deleted, the charge of Jewish culpability for the death of Jesus is rejected in the adopted Declaration. The taproots of Christianity in Judaism along with the efficacy and permanence of the Jewish covenant with God are affirmed. "Anti-Semitism" appears in *Nostra Aetate* along with calls for "mutual understanding and respect" and the establishment of "biblical and theological studies" as well as "fraternal dialogues" between Catholics and Jews.

However, Bea was aware that the hard-won document could not and did not cover all aspects of Catholic-Jewish relations, and he also recognized that it was only the first building block in constructing a new relationship with Jews. Many issues and questions remained, but Bea, Paul VI, and their late mentor John XXIII had gone as far as possible in developing that new relationship, and it was left to Spellman and Cushing to finish the long, difficult task with skill, talent, and vigor.

Future generations of Catholics and Jews would be required to give life and meaning to the tightly packed final text of *Nostra Aetate,* but a solid, hard-won foundation had been laid:

As the sacred synod searches into the mystery of the Church, it remembers the bond that spiritually ties the people of the New Covenant to Abraham's stock.

Thus the Church of Christ acknowledges that, according to God's saving design, the beginnings of her faith and her election are found already among the Patriarchs, Moses and the prophets. She professes that all who believe in Christ — Abraham's sons according to faith — are included in the same Patriarch's call, and likewise that the salvation of the Church is mysteriously foreshadowed by the chosen people's exodus from the land of bondage. The Church, therefore, cannot forget that she received the revelation of the Old Testament through the people with whom God in His inexpressible mercy concluded the Ancient Covenant. Nor can she forget that she draws sustenance from the root of that well-cultivated olive tree onto which have been grafted the wild shoots, the Gentiles. Indeed, the Church believes that by His cross Christ, Our Peace, reconciled Jews and Gentiles, making both one in Himself.

The Church keeps ever in mind the words of the Apostle about his kinsmen: "theirs is the sonship and the glory and the covenants and the law and the worship and the promises; theirs are the fathers and from them is the Christ according to the flesh" (Rom. 9:4-5), the Son of the Virgin Mary. She also recalls that the Apostles, the Church's mainstay and pillars, as well as most of the early disciples who proclaimed Christ's Gospel to the world, sprang from the Jewish people.

As Holy Scripture testifies, Jerusalem did not recognize the time of her visitation, nor did the Jews in large number, accept the Gospel; indeed not a few opposed its spreading. Nevertheless, God holds the Jews most dear for the sake of their Fathers; He does not repent of the gifts He makes or of the calls He issues — such is the witness of the Apostle. In company with the Prophets and the same Apostle, the Church awaits that day, known to God alone, on which all peoples will address the Lord in a single voice and "serve him shoulder to shoulder" (Soph. 3:9).

Since the spiritual patrimony common to Christians and Jews is thus so great, this sacred synod wants to foster and recommend that mutual understanding and respect which is the fruit, above all, of biblical and theological studies as well as of fraternal dialogues.

True, the Jewish authorities and those who followed

their lead pressed for the death of Christ; still, what happened in His passion cannot be charged against all the Jews, without distinction, then alive, nor against the Jews of today. Although the Church is the new people of God, the Jews should not be presented as rejected or accursed by God, as if this followed from the Holy Scriptures. All should see to it, then, that in catechetical work or in the preaching of the word of God they do not teach anything that does not conform to the truth of the Gospel and the spirit of Christ.

Furthermore, in her rejection of every persecution against any man, the Church, mindful of the patrimony she shares with the Jews and moved not by political reasons but by the Gospel's spiritual love, decries hatred, persecutions, displays of anti-Semitism, directed against Jews at any time and by anyone.

Besides, as the Church has always held and holds now, Christ underwent His passion and death freely, because of the sins of men and out of infinite love, in order that all may reach salvation. It is, therefore, the burden of the Church's preaching to proclaim the cross of Christ as the sign of God's all-embracing love and as the fountain from which every grace flows.

Cushing's and Spellman's interventions had guaranteed the passage of the document, but for both cardinals, *Nostra Aetate* was their final victory. Spellman died two years later in 1967 after New York State voters had rejected a referendum to provide public money for parochial schools, long one of Spellman's pet projects. Bea died a year later, and Cushing passed away in 1970. Paul VI lived until 1978; and, following the thirty-three-day pontificate of John Paul I, the College of Cardinals elected as pope a 58-year-old cardinal from Poland, Karol Wojtyla, who for the next twenty-seven years was better known as John Paul II.

CHAPTER SEVEN

The Admiral Takes Command

———⟨ѳⱮѳ⟩———

C onventional wisdom would have us believe that interreligious dialogue is a significant concern only for theological liberals; theological conservatives, it is often thought, prefer to interact with those of other faiths only by way of efforts to convert them. Yet Richard Cushing and Francis Spellman were both conservative on many issues, and so was Cardinal John O'Connor a generation later. During his tenure as archbishop of New York between 1984 and 2000, O'Connor defended his Church's opposition to abortion, same-sex marriage, capital punishment, divorce, and sex education. And he became close friends with Pope John Paul II, who also affirmed these traditional Catholic positions. Yet also like Cushing and Spellman, O'Connor worked tirelessly to improve relations between Catholics and Jews. He also supported the trade union movement, demanded a decent minimum wage for workers, assisted AIDS victims, and offered New York's mostly non-Catholic African Americans increased access to Catholic parochial schools. Then, too, despite his years as a U.S. Navy chaplain, O'Connor was a critic of many conventional military ideas and a consistent questioner of the morality of using nuclear weapons on civilian targets.

Early Years

Like many others who achieved international fame and recognition in the Big Apple, O'Connor was not a native New Yorker. He was born in Philadelphia on January 15, 1920, about one hundred miles south of Manhattan's St. Patrick's Cathedral, where he delivered sermons as archbishop and where his body is now interred. John Joseph was the fourth of five children born to Thomas and Dorothy Gomble O'Connor, both Irish immigrants to America. His father was a lifelong union member; he passed his support of organized labor down to his son: "[S]o many of our freedoms in this country," John O'Connor once preached at a Labor Day mass, "so much of the building up of society, is precisely attributable to the union movement, a movement that I personally will defend despite the weakness of some of its members, despite the corruption with which we are all familiar that pervades all society, a movement that I personally will defend with my life."

When he was 10 years old, John's mother lost her sight temporarily; her yearlong blindness sensitized the boy to the special needs of the physically disabled, and this cause became one of O'Connor's lifelong commitments. He attended public elementary school in Philadelphia, but later transferred to West Catholic High School for Boys. When he was 16, O'Connor entered Philadelphia's Catholic seminary, St. Charles Borromeo, and was ordained in 1945 at age 25. Because he was a divinity student during World War II, O'Connor was exempt from military service.

Naval Service

His first years after seminary were typical of many young Catholic clergy of the postwar era. It was a time of rapid growth for the Church, and newly ordained priests frequently were given multiple assignments. O'Connor served a parish as an assistant pastor and he also taught parochial high school classes in Chester, Pennsylvania, a city near Philadelphia. But after seven years of this life, everything changed. In 1952 Cardinal Francis Spellman issued a call for more priests to join the American armed forces. The 32-year-old Philadelphian responded to the request, embarking on a career as a Navy chaplain that would last twenty-seven years.

Over the next three decades O'Connor served both in Washington, D.C., and at sea on a guided missile cruiser. In 1964 he saw combat duty with the Third Marine Division in Vietnam, since the U.S. Marine Corps is a combat-only fighting organization and relies on the Navy for its support services. In Vietnam he earned a Legion of Merit citation and warm praise from Marine General Lewis W. Walt: "It is my opinion that no single individual in this command contributed more to the morale of the individual Marine here in Vietnam than Father O'Connor, who spent the majority of his time in the field with the men." Like many other military chaplains during the 1960s — Catholic, Jewish, and Protestant — O'Connor initially supported U.S. military involvement in Vietnam, but later changed his position. Yet his was one of the more publicized reversals, due to the fact that in 1964 he had written a book defending American military intervention in Vietnam. Years later he said that he regretted having published the book, which he characterized as "bad" and said represented "a very limited view of what was going on."

Following his tour of duty in Vietnam, O'Connor earned a master's degree in ethics and psychology at the Catholic University of America and a doctorate in political science from Georgetown University, where one of his instructors was the ardent anti-Communist Dr. Jeane Kirkpatrick, who was later the first woman to serve as U.S. ambassador to the United Nations. In 1972 O'Connor was appointed senior chaplain at the U.S. Naval Academy in Annapolis, the first Catholic to hold that position since the academy's founding in 1845.

In 1975, thirty years after becoming a priest, O'Connor was

named Chief of Navy Chaplains and promoted to the rank of rear admiral. He retired from the Navy in 1979, and by this time, because of his long military experience and his advanced degrees, he had gained the attention of the leadership of the U.S. Catholic Bishops Conference. In that same year he was consecrated a bishop and was assigned to the position Spellman held a quarter century earlier, that of overseeing Catholic chaplains in the U.S. Armed Forces.

Hawk or Dove?

In 1980 O'Connor became a member of a five-person committee headed by Cardinal Joseph Bernardin of Chicago, along with George Fulcher of Columbus, Ohio; Thomas Gumbleton of Detroit; and Daniel Reilly of Worcester, Massachusetts. The task of these five bishops was difficult and controversial: to draft a pastoral letter — that is, a Roman Catholic public statement — on the subject of nuclear arms, and the ethics and morality of using such awesome weapons. Of the five, O'Connor was the only one who had served in the military and experienced wartime combat. Yet his appointment caused consternation among anti-nuclear Catholics, who considered him a "hawk" on such issues as arms limitation, nuclear warheads, and the role of the military. They wondered whether O'Connor truly represented the Church's commitment to the cause of peace. They also worried that O'Connor, because of his military career, might overly influence other members of the drafting committee.

Yet such worry was unnecessary. By the early 1980s, the former Navy chaplain had moved away from his earlier pro-military stance. Like any good chaplain, O'Connor always expressed admiration and support for the men and women in uniform, but during the last decades of his life he became a critic of America's interventions in many parts of the world, including the *contra* guerilla campaign in Nicaragua, the missile attacks in Afghanistan, and the U.S. bombings of Kosovo in the Balkans.

In May 1983, after several years of debate and deliberation, the American bishops formally approved a pastoral letter of 64 tightly worded pages that included 127 footnotes, many of them citing the teachings of John Paul II. The document incorporated most of the committee's recommendations, and it condemned the use of nuclear weapons against civilian populations, asserting that such terrible weapons must be employed only as deterrents, and should not be used in an offensive way. Although nearly thirty years have passed since the document was adopted and it has been more than twenty years since the end of the Cold War with the former Soviet Union, this pastoral letter, titled "The Challenge to Peace," has stood the test of time, even in the current age of "asymmetrical" warfare that takes place between established nation-states and amorphous, decentralized terrorist foes.

Because of his role in the drafting of "The Challenge to Peace," in 1983 O'Connor was called to meet with John Paul II at the Vatican. The two men had much in common: they were the same age, and they were theological conservatives with warm, winning personalities that appealed to many people both in and outside the Church. And they were both attuned to the importance of building bridges of human solidarity with Jews while maintaining impeccable Catholic credentials, particularly in the pluralistic world of the late twentieth century.

The pope appointed O'Connor bishop of the Scranton, Pennsylvania, diocese, a hardscrabble, economically depressed area with a large Catholic population. (Joseph Biden, America's first Roman Catholic vice president, was born in Scranton in 1942.) And by his own account O'Connor would have been content to finish his career in this position. But he was to hold it for a mere eight and a half months. Cardinal Terence Cooke, who had succeeded Francis Spellman as archbishop of New York, died of leukemia in 1983, and O'Connor was tapped to take his place. When

in May 1985 he received his cardinal's red hat in a Vatican ceremony, John O'Connor had reached another pinnacle in his career:
first a rear admiral and Chief of U.S. Navy Chaplains with an
earned academic doctorate, and now a member of the College of
Cardinals.

A New Beginning

Many Americans retire from the workforce at 65, the age at which
John O'Connor was only beginning the most important part of his
life, the sixteen-year period when his legacy would be permanently shaped. It was a tumultuous decade and a half that transformed him, his Church, and Catholic-Jewish relations.

Looking back, it is possible to identify two factors in particular that prepared him for his extraordinary work in building positive Catholic-Jewish relations and making real the hopes and
ideals of the Second Vatican Council. First, because he grew up
in Philadelphia and later served in the armed forces, O'Connor
knew Jewish men and women as actual human beings, rather
than as an archaic, ancient "Old Testament" people or as a theological construct devoid of flesh-and-blood reality. The Philadelphia area had a Jewish population even before 1682, when it became a proprietary colony of William Penn and his family. The
city's historic Sephardic (Spanish-Portuguese) synagogue,
Mikveh Israel ("The Hope of Israel"), was formally established in
1782. One of its best known early members was the Polish-born
Hayim Solomon (1740-1785), who was a strong supporter of the
American War of Independence and a friend of many leaders of
the new nation. The city's Jewish population waxed and waned
over the years, but it is estimated that over 200,000 Jews lived in
Philadelphia in 1920, when O'Connor was born. He had Jewish
classmates in elementary school, and his Catholic high school
was in a neighborhood with a large Jewish population. Such de-

mographic facts are sometimes overlooked, but they should not be dismissed.

Second, during his long career in the Navy, O'Connor served men and women of all religious persuasions as well as those without any specific religious faith. He had years of contact with members of many faith communities, all of whom were often thrown together in combat situations. Religious pluralism was not a sociological theory or an abstract concept for O'Connor. It was what he experienced on a regular basis during his twenty-seven-year military chaplaincy.

He was thus well prepared to be archbishop in the city with America's largest Jewish population. In this role he demonstrated commitment to the survival and security of the State of Israel, understanding of the evil of the Holocaust, and support for the freedom of Soviet Jewry. Anti-Semitism was for him an affront to the Catholic faith. As one who had the pleasure of knowing him during his lifetime, I remember that he often told me, sometimes with a twinkle in his eye, of the hate mail he always received whenever he denounced anti-Semitism from the pulpit, as he often did at Sunday services. The hostile letters were an indication that he had struck a nerve among Catholics, and he was pleased to have goaded members of his flock.

Upon his arrival in New York, the new archbishop used the electronic and print media to establish himself as a refreshing new personality in a celebrity-crazed city. He conducted weekly news conferences at St. Patrick's every Sunday following Mass, a practice he continued until 1990. Witty and articulate, he was made for the sophisticated New York City media. His off-the-cuff style contrasted with that of his predecessor, Terence Cooke, who shunned the spotlight as much as possible. A particularly well-received gesture was O'Connor's standing on the front steps of St. Patrick's Cathedral to personally welcome the thousands of marchers who paraded down Fifth Avenue each spring in behalf of Soviet Jewry. Although it was a simple gesture of solidarity with the international and interreligious movement to bring freedom to the Jews in the Soviet Union, it was widely recognized as a sign of the cardinal's support for the cause.

But a firestorm of criticism erupted when O'Connor publicly equated abortion with the Holocaust, and he compounded his public relations problems during the 1984 elections when he vigorously criticized two pro-choice Catholic politicians, Governor Mario Cuomo of New York and Geraldine Ferraro, the Democratic vice presidential candidate. Yet those who hoped that O'Connor's Holocaust analogy was ill-chosen hyperbole were soon disappointed: he repeated the analogy, which ultimately resulted in a critical editorial in the *New York Times.* Because O'Connor was America's premier Catholic leader, his linking of abortion with the Holocaust angered the Jewish community. Even Orthodox rabbis who frequently agreed with O'Connor's anti-abortion stance were offended. Holocaust survivors began to sense something ominous, even threatening behind the buoyant, smiling O'Connor persona: for many survivors, he was an Americanized version of the anti-Semitic bishops they had encountered in Europe prior to and during World War II.

An Important Dinner Conversation

Here again I am able to share my own experience with Cardinal O'Connor. As the American Jewish Committee's interreligious affairs director, I became concerned about the abortion-Holocaust comparison, not only because it was inaccurate, but because it negatively affected relations between Catholics and Jews. The new archbishop was arousing tensions, and I felt something had to be done to prevent permanent damage to Catholic-Jewish relations. My opportunity to act came in 1984, during a private dinner at which O'Connor was introduced to Protestant clergy and rabbis active in interreligious activities. The otherwise friendly evening turned tense when the topic of linkage between abortion and the Holocaust was raised.

Several Christians and Jews at the dinner believed such a connection overloaded the compassion circuits, causing anger and confusion. One Protestant minister urged O'Connor to focus solely on abortion and not pair it with the Holocaust: "You are blurring two important issues." The cardinal replied that such an analogy helped draw attention to the increasing number of abortions in the nation, a trend he abhorred.

Yet at dinner's end, I had a private conversation with O'Connor. I mentioned my own military service as a United States Air Force chaplain in Japan and Korea, where a highlight of that experience was the mutual respect that existed among chaplains of various religions. Because military chaplains work in close quarters, collegiality, consultation, and shared goals are imperative. O'Connor replied that Navy chaplains serving at sea also depended upon one another for cooperation and friendship. I suggested that New York City was similar to a large military base with many religious, ethnic, and racial groups. Mutual respect and understanding were necessary if New York was to survive as a world-class city and a positive symbol of the remarkable American experiment in religious liberty and pluralism.

The cardinal nodded his head in approval, and then spoke about the Holocaust with emotion. While in the Navy, he had been traumatized by a visit he had made to the Nazi concentration camp in Dachau, near Munich. That confrontation with radical evil "changed my life forever," he told me. It was a theme he came back to many times. Like his friend John Paul II, O'Connor was gripped by the horrors of the Holocaust, a genocide carried out by baptized Christians in the heart of "civilized" Europe.

I told O'Connor that his analogy connecting abortion with the Holocaust was particularly hurtful to Holocaust survivors. Abortion, I said, is a matter of choice, however painful or regrettable. The murdered Jewish victims during the Holocaust had no choice. They were killed solely because they were Jews. I remember O'Connor's immediate response: "I would never want to harm the survivors in any way!" I urged O'Connor to "detach" his concerns and focus on abortion without attaching them to the Holocaust, and I used a military phrase we both understood: "Fight a two-front war." O'Connor thanked me for the "advice and counsel." I thought he was merely being polite, but as later events proved, that dinner encounter was the proverbial start of a beautiful friendship. Over the next sixteen years we sought out one another for advice and counsel on many issues involving Catholics and Jews.

Shortly after that dinner, O'Connor quietly abandoned the Holocaust-abortion equation in his public speeches and sermons. His critics — they were always numerous — believed he was simply being expedient. Perhaps, but I believe our one-on-one conversation helped shape O'Connor's private thinking and public advocacy. He never weakened his anti-abortion position, and at the same time he became a passionate champion of Holocaust education and remembrance. He did fight a two-front war.

A few weeks after our conversation, Cardinal O'Connor accepted my invitation to give a speech at the American Jewish Committee's 1984 annual meeting in Manhattan — twenty years after his predecessor, Cardinal Spellman, had spoken to that same organization. It was his first public appearance before a major Jewish organization since becoming New York's Catholic leader earlier that year; in it he denounced anti-Semitism and expressed his personal pain about the Holocaust. Many in the audience were surprised by O'Connor's openness, charm, and visceral hatred of anti-Semitism. I was not. I already knew that O'Connor intended to make constructive Catholic-Jewish relations a centerpiece of his work as archbishop.

A year later, in October 1985, O'Connor and I were keynote speakers at a convocation in New York City's Temple Emanu-El marking the twentieth anniversary of *Nostra Aetate*. O'Connor began his formal remarks by reading a prepared text a staffer had written. Ten minutes into the unimaginative speech, though, O'Connor literally tossed away his typewritten text and announced, "Enough of that. Now I want to really talk from my heart about Catholics and Jews." O'Connor's ad-lib remarks stirred the audience of nearly 3,000 as he spoke of the immense debt Christians owed to Jews and Judaism, and he declared that a person "cannot be a faithful Christian and an anti-Semite. They are incompatible, because anti-Semitism is a sin."

In June 1987 our friendship was again tested and strengthened when John Paul II received Kurt Waldheim, the president of Austria, at the Vatican with full diplomatic honors. At the time, the Austrian leader and former United Nations secretary general was living under an ugly public shadow because he had hidden his World War II record as a German officer in the Balkans. Waldheim was charged with being involved in the mass murder of Jews and Eastern Orthodox Christians. Because he had lied about his record for decades, the U.S. government had placed him on its watch list and barred him from entry into the United States. The warm Vatican welcome for Waldheim displeased many Jewish and Catholic leaders, including O'Connor.

"We Need You Here"

At the time of the Waldheim visit to the Vatican, I was in Hamburg, Germany, participating in an international Lutheran-Jewish conference. One night, while I was soundly asleep in my hotel room, the phone rang. Thinking the caller was someone from the front desk, I lifted the receiver and in a groggy voice mumbled, "Hullo." "Sorry if I woke you," said the familiar voice with the distinct Philadelphia accent. "Jim, I really wish you were in New York now. You could be of big help to me with the problems created by the Waldheim visit. You know, the Holy Father is planning to come to the United States in three months and plans to meet with Jewish leaders in Miami. The fallout from Waldheim's visit is all bad. It might even cancel the pope's meeting. When are you coming back? We need you here."

O'Connor was pleased when I replied, "In two days." He continued the surprising trans-Atlantic conversation, telling me he did not understand the lavish Vatican reception for Waldheim. Laughing, he said, "I intend to take it up with my friends at the Vatican." Whenever O'Connor said those words, I knew he meant only one "friend" in Rome: Pope John Paul II.

The cardinal told me the pope was also planning to visit Austria in the near future. I joked, "It's like a home and home sports event. First Waldheim comes to the Vatican, and then the pope flies to Austria." I also offered one specific suggestion: "I know the pope will visit the Mauthausen death camp near Linz, where thousands of Jews were killed. When he goes there, Waldheim must not accompany him, even if he is the Austrian president. The TV and photo images of the two men walking together would be a disaster. When the pope goes, he should visit the camp alone."

O'Connor liked the suggestion and said he would mention it to his "friends" in Rome, and apparently he did. Waldheim did not escort John Paul II to the death camp in Austria, and the solo visit to Mauthausen, along with the pope's meeting at Castel Gandolfo with Jewish leaders that summer, eased the tensions created by the Waldheim visit. In September 1987 John Paul II had a successful meeting in Miami, which I attended as one of several hundred American Jewish representatives.

I remember other times Cardinal O'Connor and I worked together on the critical issues faced by our two communities. Our friendship was a concrete result of the Second Vatican Council. In October 1965, more than 2,200 Catholic bishops adopted *Nostra Aetate,* the "Declaration on the Relationship of the Church to Non-Christian Religions," which repudiated the idea that all Jews were guilty of the death of Jesus and deplored all "hatreds, persecutions, displays of anti-Semitism" leveled at any time from any source against the Jews.

The Declaration also urged Catholics to develop "mutual understanding and respect" about Jews and Judaism, but it still required dedicated leaders like O'Connor to make *Nostra Aetate* come alive as a dynamic force within Catholicism. Without such efforts the positive work of the Second Vatican Council could easily have been relegated to the dustbins of history. The work of many Catholic and Jewish leaders might have been erased because of inaction and indifference. Fortunately, Cardinal O'Connor was neither inactive nor indifferent.

In November 1988 the cardinal spoke at a New York City synagogue to commemorate the fiftieth anniversary of the *Kristallnacht* pogrom in Germany and Austria, when in a single night hundreds of synagogues were burned and Jewish-owned stores and shops were destroyed to the sound of shattering glass windows. During *Kristallnacht,* thousands of Jews were arrested and deported to concentration camps. It marked the beginning of mass violence and murder against Jews living under Nazi rule. In his address a half century after those terrible events, O'Connor acknowledged that centuries of systematic anti-Jewish Christian teachings helped create the poisonous seedbed for Nazism. He did not flinch from the truth or attempt to pass the blame for Nazism away from traditional Christianity by laying it on "paganism."

On December 31, 1993, forty-five years after Israeli independence, the Jewish State and the Holy See finally established full diplomatic relations. To celebrate the occasion, O'Connor invited Jewish and Catholic leaders to his home behind St. Patrick's Cathedral on Madison Avenue in Manhattan. At the cardinal's reception, he asked me to offer a New Year's toast to salute the accord that had been announced a few days earlier. Raising a glass of champagne, I called O'Connor the chief architect of Vatican-Israel diplomatic relations. However, after the toast was concluded, O'Connor demurred from my words of praise. With a sly smile, the cardinal said: "No, no, Jim. The pope deserves the credit." Of course, we were both right.

In the mid-1990s, Cardinal O'Connor and I were involved in a pioneering interreligious project co-sponsored by the American Jewish Committee and the Archdiocese of New York: the Catholic-Jewish Educational Enrichment Project, C-JEEP for short. An exchange program of sorts, it offered the chance for a rabbi to become a faculty member at a Catholic high school in the city, and for a Catholic priest to do the same at a Jewish high school. It initially met some resistance from both Catholic and Jewish parents whose children attended the two schools. However, the faculties, and, above all, the students, were enthusiastic about C-JEEP because it provided not just academic content but also firsthand, personal experience of an "other." The project could not have happened without Cardinal O'Connor's support.

Humorous and jovial, O'Connor carried out his duties and responsibilities with a deft touch. Whenever I asked him how things were going, he always replied, "Every day's a holiday!" It was his way of saying how much he relished his role as one of the world's major religious figures.

Death Comes to the Cardinal

But every day was not a holiday as the cardinal neared the end of his life in the late 1990s. He had a brain tumor that required chemotherapy and other invasive treatments. But he continued his many activities despite a bleak prognosis, perhaps drawing upon the courage of his blinded mother, his religious faith, and the sense of duty he learned and practiced in the Navy.

O'Connor and I last spoke with one another in January 2000, at his residence. It was his eightieth birthday, and his face was bloated from the massive chemotherapy he had received in his losing fight against cancer. He was forced to sit in a chair as he greeted me. His once forceful handshake was no more, and when we embraced, we both knew he was terminally ill, with little time left. When O'Connor repeated his cheerful mantra about every day being a holiday, I turned away in tears. He died on May 3, 2000, but before he died, the cardinal was awarded the Congressional Gold Medal with these words: "For more than fifty years, Cardinal O'Connor has served the Catholic Church and our nation with consistency and commitment. . . . Whether it was the soldier on the battlefield or the patient dying of AIDS, Cardinal O'Connor has ministered with a gentle spirit and a loving heart. Through it all, he has stood as an advocate for the poor, a champion for workers, and an inspiration for millions."

But O'Connor always described himself with only four words: "I am a priest." Maybe so. But he is the benchmark by which all present and future Catholic priests must be judged vis-à-vis Jews and Judaism.

Over 3,500 people attended O'Connor's funeral at Saint Patrick's Cathedral, including President Bill Clinton and the First Lady, Vice President Al Gore and his wife Tipper, former President George H. W. Bush, and Texas Governor George W. Bush and his wife Laura. When the lengthy service ended, the crowd stood and loudly applauded. The clapping continued as the Cardinal's casket was slowly carried to the crypt located underneath the Cathedral's high altar, not far from Francis Spellman's final resting place.

CHAPTER EIGHT

Closing Words

———◦◦◦———

L eaders in all human endeavors who seek a positive historical legacy must be judged according to one basic question: Did they seize a never-to-be-repeated moment of opportunity and achieve genuine change, or did they allow such an opportunity to slip by?

Richard Cushing, Francis Spellman, and John O'Connor — so different from one another in style, personality, and temperament — all seized the moment and transformed the Catholic Church, moving it to higher ground in its relationship with Jews and Judaism. Although they would have denied it, these theologically conservative cardinals were, in fact, revolutionary leaders, because they were major participants in one of the greatest religious sea changes in human history.

Never Too Late to Do Good

The three men were in their sixties and seventies, and late in their long ecclesiastical careers, when they understood that although they had a limited number of years left on the world stage, there was still time enough to advance a shared vision of Catholic-

Jewish amity. They acted upon Heraclitus's famous teaching: "You cannot step twice into the same river." For Cushing and Spellman, that river was the floundering Second Vatican Council during the critical year of 1964 when the future of a strong Declaration on Jews and Judaism was in doubt. They recognized the problem and the challenge, and both vigorously stepped into that stream and changed history. O'Connor's personal river flowed much longer: the sixteen years when he was the cardinal-archbishop of New York and the most influential Catholic in the world aside from his friend and mentor, Pope John Paul II. O'Connor waded into this river and made positive Catholic-Jewish relations a centerpiece of his life and work.

It is now our generation's moment to shape and change inter-religious history, and it is important to note that Catholic-Jewish relations are far different today than they were in the days of Cushing, Spellman, and later O'Connor. Let me count the ways.

Global Warning

First, for nearly a thousand years Europe and North America have been major population centers of Christianity and Judaism. Yet during this same millennium numerous catastrophes occurred in Europe in the name of religion: the Crusades, the Inquisition, the Thirty Years War, and the culminating radical evil of the Holocaust. Yet following the end of World War II in 1945, the first successful efforts in building mutual respect and understanding between Christians and Jews took place in Europe and North America.

Second, the State of Israel, located in southwest Asia, will soon surpass the United States and become the world's largest Jewish community. Israel's Jews, many of them from Africa and Asia — including nations like Iraq, Iran, Egypt, Libya, Morocco, Syria, and Ethiopia — have had limited contact with Christians and Christianity even though papal visits to Israel by John Paul II in 2000 and Benedict XVI in 2009 helped overcome some of the emotional and psychological distance that exists between the two faith communities.

Third, the growth of Christianity, stagnant in many parts of Europe and North America, is increasing in the so-called "Third World." Catholic parishes in the U.S. have been forced to "import" priests from overseas to serve congregations of Euro-Americans. The number of candidates for the priesthood is down in the U.S., but rising in the Church's three "growth continents" of South America, Africa, and Asia. This trend will have profound and lasting impact upon future Catholic-Jewish relations.

During the nineteenth and twentieth centuries, when Catholics and Jews in the U.S. and Canada first encountered one another in large numbers, there was often suspicion, lack of authentic knowledge, hostility, and prejudice. But Catholics and Jews had at least one thing in common: they and their families, including those of Cushing, Spellman, and O'Connor, all came from Europe, and the two communities shared the difficult immigrant experience, especially in the large cities of the largely Protestant United States, where they frequently encountered anti-Semitism and anti-Catholicism in employment, housing, and education.

That close if ambivalent relationship between Catholics and Jews will not exist in the future. Catholic Church leaders with family roots in Ireland, Italy, Poland, Germany, and other European countries will be succeeded by clergy with close links to South America, Asia, and Africa. Because of history and geography, these latter Catholic groups have had little or no direct interaction with Jews — and the reverse is also true.

Also complicating the future is the inexorable march of time. Catholics and Jews who were alive and active during the tumultuous years of the Holocaust, World War II, the creation of the State of Israel, and the Second Vatican Council are passing from the scene. Their successors, some yet unborn, will be men and women who "knew not" Cushing, O'Connor, and Spellman. As a result of chronology, the next generation of Catholic leaders will feel less ownership of the Vatican Council reforms, including *Nostra Aetate*.

Unfortunately, in recent years I have met an increasing number of Catholic clergy who are unfamiliar with or even unaware of the positive interreligious developments since 1965. Often this lacuna represents omission and indifference, not malevolence or hostility. Yet the lack of accurate knowledge will accelerate unless steps are taken in colleges, universities, seminaries, and church/synagogue study programs to educate future generations about the gains of the recent past. It is ironic that Catholics and Jews, who both stress the study of history, will require special educational programs to emphasize the advances recently made between these two Peoples of God.

Yet there are several impediments to sustaining positive Catholic-Jewish relations and guaranteeing that future generations will remember and act upon the achievements of Cushing, O'Connor, Spellman, and other Catholic and Jewish leaders.

An Unresolved Controversy

One major obstacle is the continuing controversy surrounding the actions and inactions of Pope Pius XII during his pontificate, a period that included World War II, the Holocaust, the creation of the State of Israel, and the Vatican's alleged role in assisting Nazi criminals to escape punishment in the postwar period by facilitating their escape to South American safe havens. The German deportation of Rome's Jews in October 1943 to death camps took place, as the historian Susan Zuccotti titled her book, *Under His Very Windows: The Vatican and the Holocaust in Italy.* Interestingly, some Jews have joined with Catholics in defending Pius XII's wartime record and claim he saved many Jewish lives, while at the same time there are Catholic and Jewish critics of the pontiff's record.

Unless and until this dispute is brought to a mutually satisfactory conclusion, it will fester and foment suspicion and anger. One way the Vatican and other Catholic bodies can resolve this difficulty is to release all relevant archival material from the period of the Pius XII pontificate to a group of internationally recognized Catholic and Jewish scholars. Working together in the spirit of *Nostra Aetate,* the interreligious academic community can make a significant contribution to Christian-Jewish amity.

Interestingly, Cardinal O'Connor called for such action in a September 1998 speech at Clark University in Worcester, Massachusetts: "Yes, I would like to see [the archives] opened. It would be much better for the world, much better for the Church, if the archives were opened tomorrow. The pope would open everything, but not everyone in Rome is as open-minded."

Concerns about Benedict XVI

Another problem is the sense shared by a number of Catholics and Jews that Pope Benedict XVI may lack the passion and commitment of his predecessor to break new ground in Catholic-Jewish relations. Critics charge that he generally seems content to stand on the gains of the past. One reason for this belief is the pope's mishandled efforts in early 2009, when he lifted the excommunications of five "bishops" of the ultra-conservative Society of St. Pius X, a group John Paul II had excommunicated twenty years earlier in 1988.

One Society "bishop," Richard Williamson of Britain, is a prominent public Holocaust denier. Benedict's action created a firestorm of criticism and a sense of anger among many Catholics and Jews. The initial Vatican response was defensive, that the pope did not know of Williamson's statements, writings, and television interviews that denied the reality of the mass murder of six million Jews. However, when it was pointed out that such information about Williamson and his obscene views was readily available on the Internet, Benedict XVI, in a rare action for a pope, publicly apologized. The pontiff said he made a mistake in announcing his actions without checking Williamson's public record, which included a widely viewed European television interview in which he denied the historical reality of the Holocaust. In March 2009 Benedict wrote,

> An unforeseen mishap for me was the fact that the Williamson case . . . momentarily upset peace between Christians and Jews, as well as peace within the Church; [it] is something which I can only deeply deplore. I have been told that consulting the information available on the Internet would have made it possible to perceive the problem early on. I have learned the lesson that in the future in the Holy See we will have to pay greater attention to that source of news. I was saddened by the fact that even Catholics who, after all, might have had a better knowledge of the situation, thought they had to attack me with open hostility. Precisely for this reason I thank all the more our Jewish friends, who quickly helped to clear up the misunderstanding and to restore the atmosphere of friendship and trust which — as in the days of Pope John Paul II — has also existed throughout my pontificate and, thank God, continues to exist.

A year later the issue was still in Benedict's mind when he told an interviewer, "If I had known, the first step would have been to separate the Williamson case from the others. Unfortunately, though, none of us went on the Internet to find out what sort of person we were dealing with. . . . On our side, it was a mistake not to have studied and prepared the case more carefully."

While Benedict has visited some of the same locations as his predecessor — Jewish houses of worship, including the Great Synagogue in Rome, the Auschwitz death camp, and the state of Israel — and despite the pope's positive statements, critics wonder: Will John Paul II's historic achievements and teachings about Jews and Judaism be further strengthened by Benedict? Or will they be weakened as Catholics increasingly turn inward because of the widespread clergy sexual abuse scandal? Or will relations with Judaism be sidelined by the need to devote more Church attention to Islam and its more than one billion adherents?

Critics further charge that Benedict is vitiating Vatican Council reforms. His defenders reject such charges and assert the reforms adopted by the world's bishops in the 1960s are not susceptible to repeal. They also point out the centerpiece of Benedict's papal agenda is to halt the defection of Catholics, especially in Europe, to indifference and secularism, and to restore traditional faith and liturgy to a prominent place among Catholics. Yet other critics charge the Vatican with promoting a kind of benign neglect of Jewish-Catholic relations.

Still others wonder whether it is time for both faith communities to pause after nearly a half century of enormous energy, and perhaps take a time out to consolidate the extraordinary gains. But such a belief prevents both Catholics and Jews from moving ahead; a hiatus is fraught with danger. Leaving either a car or a set of relations in neutral produces no forward motion, and in the case of human behavior once positive relationships can atrophy or disappear if left unattended.

Does the work of Richard Cushing, Francis Spellman, and John O'Connor yet have meaning today? Do these three cardinals still merit our attention? Other questions remain: Why did the three leaders devote so much of their religious capital to the cause of positive Catholic-Jewish relations? Why did they risk their already secure reputations and their future places in history to advocate radical reforms they knew meant confronting entrenched thinking and traditional behavior among their peers and many of the men and women in the parish pews? And why did this trio break so sharply with the past and demand that the Catholic Church permanently change its relationship with Jews and Judaism?

The best answer to these questions comes from a cardinal who was always modest about his academic, linguistic, and theological abilities; an indifferent student who was a high school and college dropout before becoming a priest; a cardinal who was the most self-effacing of the trio portrayed in this book; a cardinal who during his lifetime was belittled by many of his flock and ecclesiastical colleagues, but who at the same time was also beloved and treasured by many others both inside and outside the Church.

"Too Large for Enmity, Too Small for Isolationism"

On February 24, 1964, an alarmed Cardinal Richard Cushing sent an impassioned letter to Cardinal Augustin Bea, the Vatican official who led the efforts to adopt a positive Declaration on Jews and Judaism. The Boston archbishop wrote his fellow prince of the Church:

> I am no theologian and I am not a scholar, but I am very close to people of all faiths. Unless the Council comes forth with a statement concerning the right of every individual to worship God in accordance with the dictates of his conscience, and with a statement relative to the fact that all mankind is responsible for the death of Christ, and not a few Jews and Roman soldiers, the ecumenical spirit will be meaningless, in so far as the Catholic Church is concerned.
>
> We have a wonderful opportunity in the pluralistic society of the United States to create the greatest good will for the Catholic Church and the greatest climate . . . the Church has lived in [during] the past four hundred years.

On November 10, 1964, only six weeks after his intervention at the Vatican Council, Cushing wrote a letter to Alan Shactman, a Boston insurance executive and a prominent member of that city's Jewish community and a leader of B'nai Brith, a national Jewish fraternal organization. It was a response to Shactman's earlier note congratulating Cushing for his September 28 speech in Rome. But the Jewish layman remained concerned about the uncertain status of *Nostra Aetate*. The cardinal reassured his Jewish friend:

> Let me say these two statements ["Religious Liberty" and *Nostra Aetate*] will definitely . . . be promulgated [even though] the special consideration of the Jews will be misinterpreted as a political maneuver. The Arab and Moslem nations will interpret this as preferential favor toward the State of Israel and will subject Christian minorities to persecution. . . . Christians in the Middle East have long lived by a tenuous toleration of the Moslem majorities. . . . I pray the final form will move all Catholics to greater love of their fellow-men, encourage the dialogue of the Church with other Churches and religions, hasten the unity and harmony of all men in our modern world which is too large for enmity, too small for isolationism.

Why devote such energy, such time, such resources to improving Catholic-Jewish relations? No one has ever said it better than the blacksmith's son from South Boston.

Index